Teaching Guide Stages 1–3

CONTENTS

Introducing *Rapid*

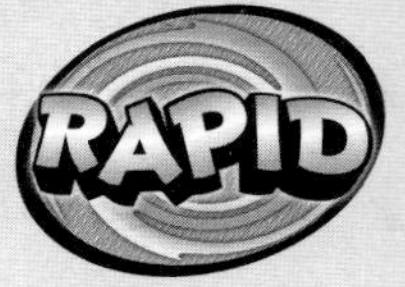

The *Rapid* programme is a collection of resources to support you in your work with children who find reading difficult. It provides:

- finely-levelled fiction and non-fiction readers
- motivating speech recognition software for reading practice
- assessment texts to monitor pupils' reading progress
- photocopiable worksheets to consolidate word-level work
- lesson plans for Guided Reading sessions
- guidance and teaching support, within the readers and this Teaching Guide.

Who are the target pupils?

The *Rapid* programme provides the small but important steps which will move struggling readers aged 7–11 years from a reading age of 5.6 to a reading age of 8+.

The *Rapid* texts

The *Rapid* texts are high-interest stories and motivating non-fiction topics which will inspire struggling readers. Each text is a whole reading experience. The text is always introduced by means of a *Before Reading* page which sets the scene, introduces the characters or topic, and launches the pupil into independent reading. The text is then followed by a *Quiz* page which invites the pupil to revisit the text, and helps to develop comprehension and word-level skills. Each *Rapid* text has been developed to ensure that pupils make steady progress in their reading. Some of the features which ensure this progress are:

- Limited number of different words within each text.
- Thematically-linked fiction and non-fiction texts, within one book.
- Fiction texts within each Set share the same main characters.
- Short texts, designed for a 10-minute reading intervention session, or a Guided Reading session.
- Chunked text boxes divide the text, to ensure that pages do not look too daunting for pupils.
- *Rapid* texts use a specially-designed font to help the struggling reader make the important distinctions between confusable letters such as 'b' and 'd'.
- The phonic activities on the *Quiz* pages direct pupils back to words in the text to analyse them for phonic features.

The *Rapid* texts and 'Wave 3'

The DfES has identified children who need individual support for reading and writing as 'Wave 3' pupils. It is acknowledged that if these pupils are to 'catch up' with their peers, they will need to make double the rate of normal progress. *Rapid*, with its careful progression, will be a key tool in helping children to achieve this.

How should I hear a pupil read?

Research suggests that adopting a consistent approach when hearing pupils read builds the confidence of struggling readers. An effective strategy to use is the Pause, Prompt and Praise procedure:

1. **PAUSE** up to eight seconds, to give the pupil 'thinking time'.
2. If the pupil is still unable to decode the word, then the adult should provide a **PROMPT**, based on the quickest route to decoding the word.
3. The adult should also **PRAISE** pupils. Frequent praise will provide the incentive the pupil needs to persevere with the challenge of reading.

Based on *The Pause, Prompt and Praise Tutoring Procedure*, Wheldall et al. 1981

Hearing a pupil read a *Rapid* text

BEFORE READING

Introduce the Reading Book to the pupil and, using page 1 of the book, ask them to select the text they wish to read – fiction, or non-fiction.

Read the *Before Reading* page together:

- Talk about the characters or the 'Find out about' section.
- Point to and read the tricky words together.
- Read the title together.
- Give a lively reading of the Story/Text starter to launch the pupil into the reading.

READING THE TEXT

- Allow the pupil to read on independently.
- Employ the **Pause and Prompt** strategies.
- If the pupil stumbles on a tricky word or the name of a character, be prepared to support their reading.
- **Praise** the pupil when they are successful and also when they demonstrate good decoding strategies.

AFTER READING

Read the *Quiz* page together:

- Read the *Text Detective* questions to the pupil. Encourage them to give full answers.
- Read the *Word Detective* questions to the pupil. Encourage them to listen carefully to the *Phonic Focus*. Revisit the relevant pages and encourage them to find the focus words.
- Provide a notebook for each pupil. Read the *Super Speller* words to the pupil and allow them to study each word. Then cover the words and ask them to write each word in turn.

Key features of *Rapid*

- **In this story / Find out about:** Familiarises the pupil with the characters' names in fiction texts and key concepts in non-fiction texts.

- **High-interest stories and themes:** The *Rapid* texts are specifically chosen to appeal to older struggling readers. The stories are fast-paced and the information texts are either amazing or revolting – and sometimes both!

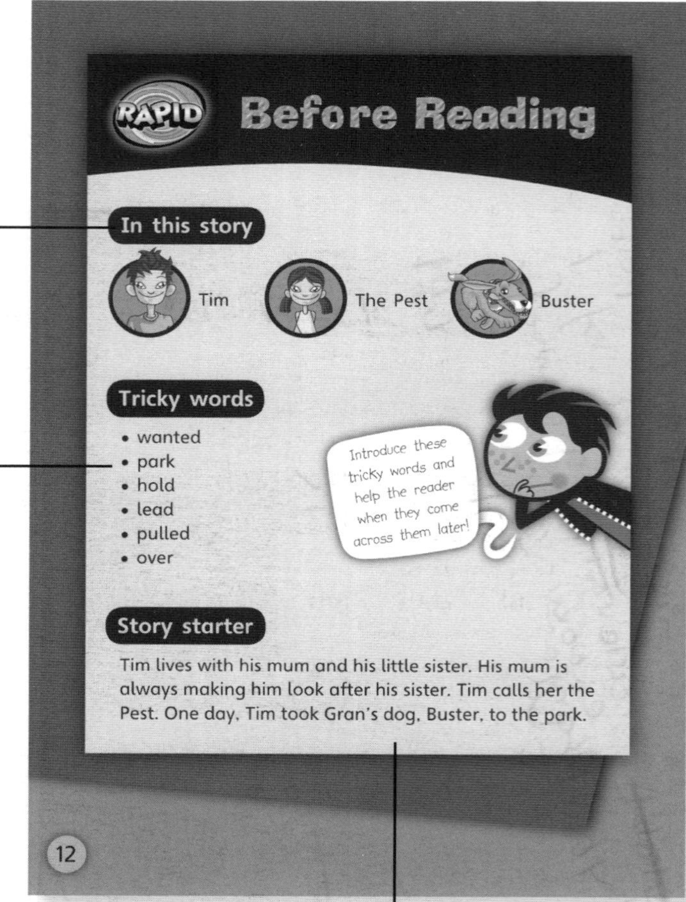

- **Tricky words:** These are words that are specific to the text about to be read, and which are likely to be unfamiliar to the pupil.

- **Story / Text starter:** 'Launches' the pupil into the reading. The purpose of this is to set the context for the pupil so that they have 'the big picture' of the text clearly in their minds before they start reading.

- **Text boxes:** The text boxes are presented with a cream background. This avoids the sharp contrast between black print and a white background.

- **Simple language:** The texts avoid sentence complexity which so easily confuses the struggling reader.

- **Striking design and artwork:** Guaranteed to appeal to the older struggling reader.

- **Linked vocabulary:** Linking a fiction text with a non-fiction text in the same book allows the reader to meet the same vocabulary in different contexts.

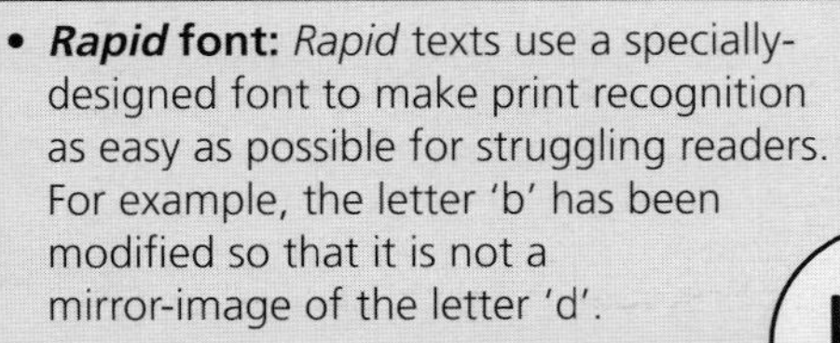

- ***Rapid* font:** *Rapid* texts use a specially-designed font to make print recognition as easy as possible for struggling readers. For example, the letter 'b' has been modified so that it is not a mirror-image of the letter 'd'.

bd

Buster was a big dog. He pulled and pulled on the lead.

He pulled Tim, too!

What do you think is going to happen next?

15

- **Chunked text:** At Stages 1–3, *Rapid* text is set out in linked boxes. The purpose of this is to present manageable chunks of reading. Struggling readers can easily be daunted by text which appears to 'float' on the page and they can lose their place when reading.

- **Cartoon character:** Throughout the texts, a series cartoon character (*Rapid Boy!*) appears with comments and questions to challenge the reader. This device ensures pupils engage in prediction and reflection.

- **Text Detective:** Checks the pupil's comprehension through literal and inferential questions, and personal response.

- **Word Detective:** Directs the pupil back into the text to find examples of particular phonic features.

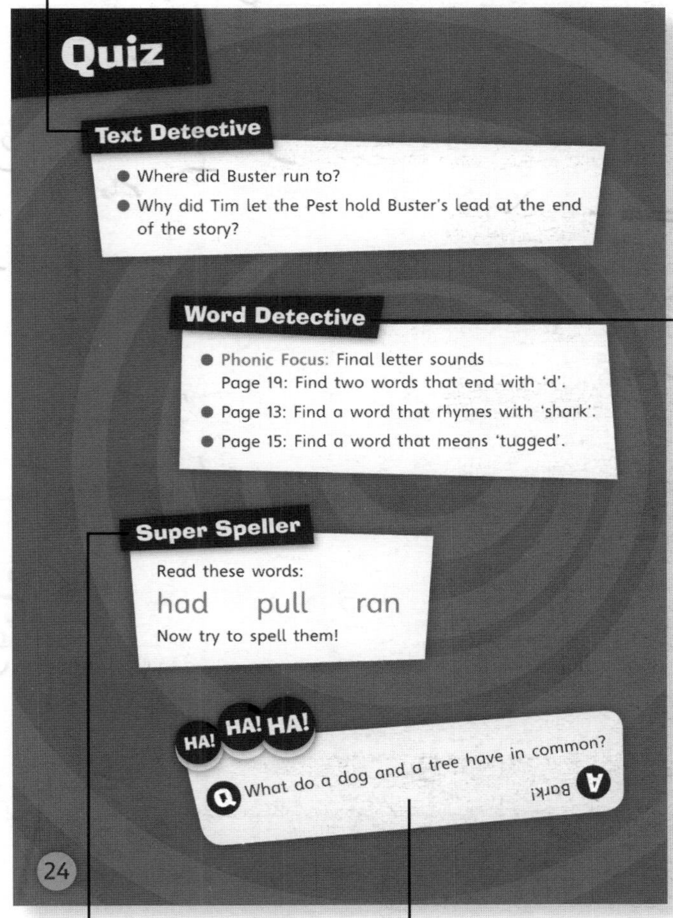

- **Super Speller:** Makes links between reading and spelling and encourages pupils to study words they have met in the text, and then to practise spelling these words from memory.

- **Joke:** Finally, each *Quiz* page ends with a joke which links thematically with the text. A brilliant way to round off a reading experience!

Programme overview

Stage	Reading Books	*Reading Assistant* Software	Assessment Books	Teaching Guides
Stage 1 NC 1C 5–14 A NI → 2	Set A Set B	Stages 1–3	Set A Set B	Stages 1–3
Stage 2 NC 1B 5–14 A NI → 2	Set A Set B		Set A Set B	
Stage 3 NC 1A 5–14 → B NI 2	Set A Set B		Set A Set B	
Stage 4 NC 2C 5–14 → B NI 2	Set A Set B	Stages 4–6	Set A Set B	Stages 4–6
Stage 5 NC 2B 5–14 B NI 2	Set A Set B		Set A Set B	
Stage 6 NC 2A/3C 5–14 → C NI 2	Set A Set B		Set A Set B	

KEY
- NC = England and Wales National Curriculum Level
- 5–14 = Scottish 5–14 Level
- NI = Northern Ireland Curriculum Level
- → = Towards
- ◤ = Non-fiction ◢ = Fiction

Placing a pupil within the programme

For many pupils, the starting point within *Rapid* will be Stage 1 Set A. From this beginning they will make steady progress through to Stage 6 Set B.

If Stage 1 Set A is not a suitable starting point for a pupil, you can use the following table to determine the entry point to *Rapid*. Then use the 'scope and sequence' charts on pages 11–16 to decide which Stage (1–6), and in which Set (A or B) a pupil should be placed.

Rapid Level	Reading Age	England and Wales National Curriculum Level	Scottish 5–14 Level	Northern Ireland Curriculum Level	*Catch Up Level
Stage 1 Set A or B	5.6 – 5.11	1C	Within Level A	Towards Level 2	4
Stage 2 Set A or B	6.0 – 6.5	1B	Within Level A	Towards Level 2	5
Stage 3 Set A or B	6.6 – 6.11	1A	Towards Level B	Within Level 2	6
Stage 4 Set A or B	7.0 – 7.5	2C	Towards Level B	Within Level 2	7
Stage 5 Set A or B	7.6 – 7.11	2B	Within Level B	Within Level 2	8
Stage 6 Set A or B	8.0 – 8.5	2A/3C	Towards Level C	Within Level 2	9

Catch Up* is a structured literacy intervention programme for pupils in Years 2–8. For more information see **www.catchup.org.uk

Using the Assessment Books to place a pupil within the programme
Another way to place a pupil within the *Rapid* programme is to use the Assessment Books at each Stage of the programme. You will find a section on *Rapid* Assessment on pages 91–111 of this Teaching Guide, which describes the purpose of the Assessment Books as summative assessment, i.e. for use *after* a pupil has read all four Reading Books in a Set. However, the Assessment Books can also be used to help to **place a pupil within *Rapid*** by asking a pupil to read the assessment text from the Stage below the level at which the pupil is reading. For example, if a pupil has a reading age of 6 years 6 months, use the assessment text from Stage 2 Set B to confirm the pupil is confidently reading at this level. If the prediction is confirmed, then start the pupil on Stage 3 Set A.

Rapid: The whole solution

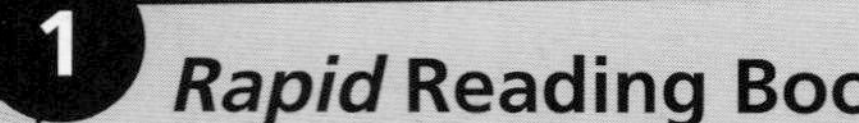

1 *Rapid* Reading Books

Within each reading book, there are two thematically-linked texts; one fiction and one non-fiction. Whether you are using the books for one-on-one intervention, or Guided Reading, choose just **one** text per reading session.

Intervention reading: For guidance on how to use the *Rapid* texts for a one-on-one reading session, see the notes on pages 3–5 of this Guide.

Guided Reading: For guidance on how to use the *Rapid* texts for Guided Reading sessions, see the notes on pages 17–18 of this Guide. There are comprehensive Guided Reading notes, which support **every** *Rapid* text, from page 19 onwards (preceding the photocopy master (PCM) worksheets for each text).

Follow-up work
After each text there is also the opportunity to give the pupil follow-up work. Each *Rapid* book is accompanied by two photocopy master (PCM) worksheets. One PCM supports phonic skills, whilst the other focuses on writing skills.

When a child is ready to move up to the next Set of the *Rapid* programme, the process of using reading books, software and assessment begins again.

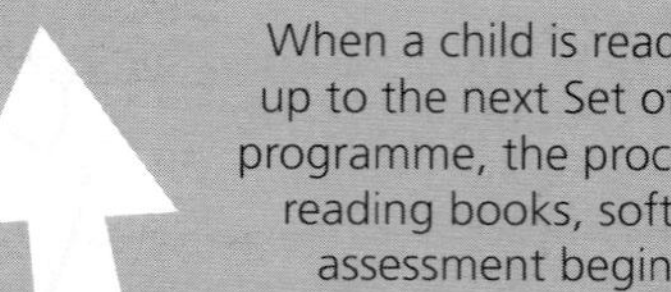

3 *Rapid* Assessment

The *Rapid* programme has an integral assessment strand, which can be used to:

- place the pupil within the programme
- check whether the pupil is ready to move up to the next Set of the programme
- provide ongoing tracking of the pupil's reading performance.

There is one Assessment Book for every Stage of the *Rapid* programme. Each book contains two fiction texts which are used to assess the pupil's success with each Set at that Stage. For example, the Stage 1 Assessment Book contains one text which is used to assess Stage 1 Set A, and another text which is used to assess Stage 1 Set B.

Once a child has read all four books in one Set (that's eight texts) they are ready to be assessed on the vocabulary and reading skills learned during their reading, using the Assessment Books.

All the support needed to use these Assessment Books, can be found on pages 91–111 of this Teaching Guide.

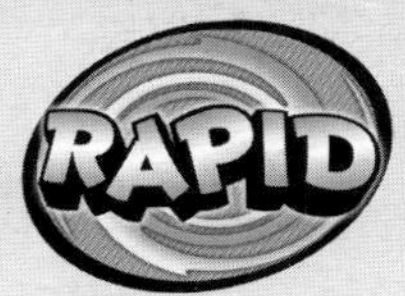

The pupil continues reading the *Rapid* Reading Books and using the *Rapid Reading Assistant* software, until all eight texts within a Set are completed.

2 *Rapid Reading Assistant* Software

Once a pupil has read a text from the *Rapid* Reading Books, they can practise reading that text again, using the *Rapid Reading Assistant* software. This speech recognition software has two main features:

Read to Me: A pupil can listen to a *Rapid* text being read on screen. This reinforcement of the text helps them with understanding and fluency. You can choose to use the 'Read to Me' feature before a pupil reads a text for the first time, if you feel the previewing of a text would build confidence before a reading session.

Read and Record: A pupil can then independently read the text again, recording this reading as they go. If they stumble on any word, the software will prompt and guide them through the reading. This feature allows the pupil to play back their own reading, as well as providing both pupil and teacher with a wealth of information on the pupil's reading performance.

The teaching support for using the *Rapid Reading Assistant* software is provided alongside the software itself. To find out more about this software, visit **www.myprimary.co.uk/rapid**

Getting Started: Your Questions Answered

Do the books in a Set need to be read in a particular order?

No! Each Set of four books can be read in any order, as there is no difference in the level of reading difficulty.

How often should I be using *Rapid* with a pupil?

Ideally, a struggling reader will benefit from having two one-on-one sessions per week. This could be followed up by the pupil completing Follow-up PCMs, and using the *Rapid Reading Assistant* software.

How do I keep track of all of the pupil's work with *Rapid*?

Creating a document-wallet for each pupil enables you to keep all relevant paperwork together. This could include:

- *Super Speller* notebook
- Assessment sheets
- Follow-up PCM worksheets
- Software reports.

If your question about the *Rapid* programme has not been answered here or elsewhere in the Teaching Guide, please see our website **www.myprimary.co.uk/rapid** for further information, including video clips of resources being used in the classroom, or for customer service details.

The structure of the programme

The *Rapid* programme comprises 48 Reading Books divided into six Stages of reading development. Each book contains one fiction and one non-fiction text, which are thematically-linked. This gives a total of 96 carefully-levelled reading experiences.

How is the levelling achieved?

- **Controlling the number of words:** Each text has a maximum number of total words and a specified maximum number of different words (see pages 11–16). For example, each text in Stage 1 Set A has a maximum of 30 different words, and 100 words in total. Each text in Stage 3 Set B has a maximum of 75 different words, and 220 words in total. The pupil therefore frequently meets the same words across different texts, and this continuity builds reading confidence.
- **High-frequency words:** Each text is written using as many as possible of the first 100 high-frequency words. Unfamiliar words are introduced to the pupil in the *Before Reading* page as 'Tricky words'. This device enables the pupil to concentrate on reading the high-frequency words without being distracted by less familiar words. (See pages 11–16.)
- **Phonological knowledge:** Whilst the texts are not written to a phonic formula, the *Word Detective* activities on the *Quiz* page direct the pupil back to words in the text to analyse them for phonic features, e.g. initial and final phoneme, and medial vowel. Activities such as blending three phonemes build on and consolidate phonic knowledge in a systematic and progressive way. (See the charts on pages 11–16.)
- **Spelling knowledge:** Three high-frequency words have been selected from each text for spelling practice. These are identified in the *Super Speller* on the *Quiz* page. The pupils are directed to study the words and then spell them from memory.
- **Development of comprehension:** The *Quiz* page at the end of each text has two questions to assess comprehension, under the heading of *Text Detective*. The first question requires an answer that draws on a literal recall of events in the text. The second question requires inferential comprehension, either in the form of reading between the lines, or making a personal response. As the texts progress in difficulty, so the questions become more searching.
- **Progression in text layout:** *Rapid* Stages 1–3 displays texts in a series of linked text boxes. This helps the uncertain reader to hold on to chunks of meaning, linked to each sentence. At Stages 4–6, the text is presented in discrete boxes. This progression in layout reflects the pupil's growing confidence and ability in handling larger chunks of text.

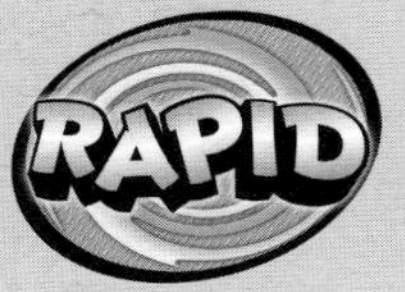

***Rapid* Level**	Stage 1 Set A
Curriculum Level	NC 1C / 5–14 Within Level A / NI Towards Level 2
Reading Age	5.6 – 5.11

Maximum number of different words:
30

Maximum number of total words:
100

Phonic Focus:
Initial letter sounds

Literacy Targets for Stage 1 Set A

Recall and Response (Text Detective)

- Simple literal recall of events or facts
- Personal response to story

Word recognition and phonic knowledge (Word Detective)

- Initial letter sounds
- Finding rhyming words
- Recognising high-frequency words

Spelling knowledge (Super Speller)

- Spelling two- and three-letter high-frequency words

Key Words for Stage 1 Set A

- at
- in
- is
- it
- on
- and
- had
- did
- yes
- me

Super Snakes

Sneaky Pete

Fiction

Number of different words: 30

Phonic Focus:
Initial letter sounds – t

Super Speller words:
• but • see • to

Snake Bites

Non-fiction

Number of different words: 29

Phonic Focus:
Initial letter sounds – b

Super Speller words:
• and • it • of

Trunk Tales

Naughty Nellie

Fiction

Number of different words: 29

Phonic Focus:
Initial letter sounds – ch

Super Speller words:
• did • not • the

Elephants

Non-fiction

Number of different words: 30

Phonic Focus:
Initial letter sounds – th

Super Speller words:
• big • can • is

Chimps and Us

Are You Like a Chimpanzee?

Non-fiction

Number of different words: 28

Phonic Focus:
Initial letter sounds – h

Super Speller words:
• do • eat • so

Cheeky Charlie

Fiction

Number of different words: 30

Phonic Focus:
Initial letter sounds – ch

Super Speller words:
• he • my • on

Big Cats, Small Cats

Are Lions like Cats?

Non-fiction

Number of different words: 26

Phonic Focus:
Initial letter sounds – l

Super Speller words:
• at • has • like

Lazy Leo

Fiction

Number of different words: 30

Phonic Focus:
Initial letter sounds – g

Super Speller words:
• get • up • will

***Rapid* Level** Stage 1 Set B

Curriculum Level NC 1C / 5–14 Within Level A / NI Towards Level 2

Reading Age 5.6 – 5.11

Maximum number of different words:
36

Maximum number of total words:
120

Phonic Focus:
Final letter sounds

Literacy Targets for Stage 1 Set B

Recall and Response (Text Detective)
- Simple literal recall of events or facts
- Personal response to story

Word recognition and phonic knowledge (Word Detective)
- Final letter sounds
- Finding rhyming words
- Recognising high-frequency words

Spelling knowledge (Super Speller)
- Spelling simple high-frequency words

Key Words for Stage 1 Set B

- he
- go
- to
- the
- got
- but
- can
- will
- was
- not

Chocolate Chunks

Tim, the Pest and the Chocolate Robber
Fiction

Number of different words: 36

Phonic Focus:
Final letter sounds – k

Super Speller words:
• fell • got • put

Chocolate World
Non-fiction

Number of different words: 34

Phonic Focus:
Final letter sounds – n

Super Speller words:
• in • was • you

Daring Dogs

Dogs to the Rescue
Non-fiction

Number of different words: 33

Phonic Focus:
Final letter sounds – g

Super Speller words:
• find • help • some

Tim, the Pest and the Big Dog
Fiction

Number of different words: 35

Phonic Focus:
Final letter sounds – d

Super Speller words:
• had • pull • ran

Monsters!

Tim, the Pest and the Ice Monster
Fiction

Number of different words: 35

Phonic Focus:
Final letter sounds – th

Super Speller words:
• her • his • saw

Monsters on Film
Non-fiction

Number of different words: 29

Phonic Focus:
Final letter sounds – m

Super Speller words:
• are • just • makes

Sports Mad

Match Crazy!
Non-fiction

Number of different words: 34

Phonic Focus:
Final letter sounds – t

Super Speller words:
• off • one • sent

Tim, the Pest and the Footballer
Fiction

Number of different words: 35

Phonic Focus:
Final letter sounds – p

Super Speller words:
• new • out • she

***Rapid* Level**	Stage 2 Set A
Curriculum Level	NC 1B / 5–14 Within Level A / NI Towards Level 2
Reading Age	6.0 – 6.5

Maximum number of different words:
40

Maximum number of total words:
140

Phonic Focus:
Blending three phonemes

Literacy Targets for Stage 2 Set A

Recall and Response (Text Detective)
- Literal recall of events or facts
- Personal response to story

Word recognition and phonic knowledge (Word Detective)
- Blending three-letter words
- Recognising high-frequency words
- Vocabulary extension – finding words of similar meaning

Spelling knowledge (Super Speller)
- Spelling high-frequency words

Key Words for Stage 2 Set A

- big
- see
- has
- saw
- his
- said
- with
- him
- like
- here
- you
- stop
- out
- have
- all

Pedal Power

On Your Bike!

Fiction

Number of different words: 40

Phonic Focus:
Blending three phonemes

Super Speller words:
• too • going • went

All Kinds of Bikes

Non-fiction

Number of different words: 40

Phonic Focus:
Blending three phonemes

Super Speller words:
• be • must • they

Just the Job!

Crazy Jobs

Non-fiction

Number of different words: 40

Phonic Focus:
Blending three phonemes

Super Speller words:
• have • more • very

I Want a New Bike!

Fiction

Number of different words: 40

Phonic Focus:
Blending three phonemes

Super Speller words:
• for • gave • hard

Do You Believe It?

Real Snowmen

Non-fiction

Number of different words: 40

Phonic Focus:
Blending three phonemes

Super Speller words:
• made • say • think

The Old Skateboard

Fiction

Number of different words: 40

Phonic Focus:
Blending three phonemes

Super Speller words:
• come • stop • want

Don't Drop It!

Star-struck Tom

Fiction

Number of different words: 38

Phonic Focus:
Blending three phonemes

Super Speller words:
• day • man • played

How to Juggle

Non-fiction

Number of different words: 37

Phonic Focus:
Blending three phonemes

Super Speller words:
• from • now • your

***Rapid* Level**	Stage 2 Set B
Curriculum Level	NC 1B / 5–14 Within Level A / NI Towards Level 2
Reading Age	6.0 – 6.5

Maximum number of different words:
50

Maximum number of total words:
160

Phonic Focus:
Blending three phonemes

Literacy Targets for Stage 2 Set B

Recall and Response (Text Detective)

- Literal recall of events or facts
- Personal response to story

Word recognition and phonic knowledge (Word Detective)

- Hearing medial vowel in three-letter words
- Recognising high-frequency words
- Vocabulary extension – finding words of similar meaning

Spelling knowledge (Super Speller)

- Spelling high-frequency words

Key Words for Stage 2 Set B

• are	• some	• this
• very	• want	• get
• down	• went	• that
• must	• came	• old
• our	• they	• into

Creepy Castles

Sir Bold and the Haunted Castle	**Castles**
Fiction	Non-fiction
Number of different words: 43	**Number of different words:** 50
Phonic Focus: Blending three phonemes	**Phonic Focus:** Blending three phonemes
Super Speller words: • here • old • said	**Super Speller words:** • hill • into • look

Dragons

Today's Dragons	**Sir Bold and the Dragon**
Non-fiction	Fiction
Number of different words: 42	**Number of different words:** 47
Phonic Focus: Blending three phonemes	**Phonic Focus:** Blending three phonemes
Super Speller words: • fly • looks • this	**Super Speller words:** • didn't • read • with

Knights and Fights

Sir Bold and the Tournament	**Knights and their Weapons**
Fiction	Non-fiction
Number of different words: 41	**Number of different words:** 43
Phonic Focus: Blending three phonemes	**Phonic Focus:** Blending three phonemes
Super Speller words: • first • our • that	**Super Speller words:** • down • fall • how

Treasure!

The Search for the Treasure of Tutankhamen	**Sir Bold and the Gold Cup**
Non-fiction	Fiction
Number of different words: 48	**Number of different words:** 49
Phonic Focus: Blending three phonemes	**Phonic Focus:** Blending three phonemes
Super Speller words: • all • then • two	**Super Speller words:** • came • there • took

***Rapid* Level**	Stage 3 Set A
Curriculum Level	NC 1A / 5–14 Towards Level B / NI Within Level 2
Reading Age	6.6 – 6.11

Maximum number of different words:
60

Maximum number of total words:
180

Phonic Focus:
Initial consonant clusters

Literacy Targets for Stage 3 Set A

Recall and Response (Text Detective)

- Literal recall of events or facts
- Personal response to story

Word recognition and phonic knowledge (Word Detective)

- Blending consonant clusters in initial position
- Recognising high-frequency words
- Chunking longer words into syllables

Spelling knowledge (Super Speller)

- Spelling high-frequency words

Key Words for Stage 3 Set A

- were
- put
- one
- looked
- for
- away
- off
- wanted
- lots
- does
- most
- think
- gave
- then
- fast
- coming
- jumped
- would
- now
- open

Huge and Hairy

Bigfoot

Non-fiction

Number of different words: 59

Phonic Focus:
Initial consonant clusters

Super Speller words:
• after • away • huge

Jack and the Mountain

Fiction

Number of different words: 58

Phonic Focus:
Initial consonant clusters

Super Speller words:
• climb • coming • fast

Beyond the Stars

Jack on Planet Spot

Fiction

Number of different words: 58

Phonic Focus:
Initial consonant clusters

Super Speller words:
• could • jumped • were

The Planets

Non-fiction

Number of different words: 60

Phonic Focus:
Initial consonant clusters

Super Speller words:
• night • school • would

Savage Beasts

Jack in Africa

Fiction

Number of different words: 54

Phonic Focus:
Initial consonant clusters

Super Speller words:
• boat • sleep • wanted

Fierce Animals

Non-fiction

Number of different words: 52

Phonic Focus:
Initial consonant clusters

Super Speller words:
• bite • does • kill

Under the Sea

Funny, Weird and Scary

Non-fiction

Number of different words: 57

Phonic Focus:
Initial consonant clusters

Super Speller words:
• funny • light • lives

Jack and the Wreck

Fiction

Number of different words: 60

Phonic Focus:
Initial consonant clusters

Super Speller words:
• lots • open • over

***Rapid* Level**	Stage 3 Set B
Curriculum Level	NC 1A / 5–14 Towards Level B / NI Within Level 2
Reading Age	6.6 – 6.11

Maximum number of different words:
75

Maximum number of total words:
220

Phonic Focus:
Final consonant clusters

Literacy Targets for Stage 3 Set B

Recall and Response (Text Detective)
- Literal recall of events or facts
- Personal response to story

Word recognition and phonic knowledge (Word Detective)
- Blending consonant clusters in final position
- Finding words of similar meaning
- Chunking longer words into syllables

Spelling knowledge (Super Speller)
- Spelling high-frequency words

Key Words for Stage 3 Set B

- could
- full
- more
- from
- made
- your
- their
- eat
- again
- so
- where
- took
- what
- live
- home
- who
- her
- there
- just
- half

Big Bangs!

Jim and the Fireworks

Fiction

Number of different words: 74

Phonic Focus:
Final consonant clusters

Super Speller words:
• again • couldn't • their

Volcanoes

Non-fiction

Number of different words: 72

Phonic Focus:
Final consonant clusters

Super Speller words:
• called • what • when

What a Monster!

Make-Believe Monsters

Non-fiction

Number of different words: 72

Phonic Focus:
Final consonant clusters

Super Speller words:
• half • kind • who

Treasure Island

Fiction

Number of different words: 73

Phonic Focus:
Final consonant clusters

Super Speller words:
• blew • crept • swam

Jelly Trouble!

Give Us Our Ship Back!

Fiction

Number of different words: 75

Phonic Focus:
Final consonant clusters

Super Speller words:
• back • cried • mend

Jellyfish

Non-fiction

Number of different words: 63

Phonic Focus:
Final consonant clusters

Super Speller words:
• great • other • tiny

Ship Shape

Life at Sea

Non-fiction

Number of different words: 74

Phonic Focus:
Final consonant clusters

Super Speller words:
• fight • food • long

The Treasure Map

Fiction

Number of different words: 70

Phonic Focus:
Final consonant clusters

Super Speller words:
• can't • found • where

Guided Reading Notes and Photocopy Master Worksheets

The *Rapid* Reading Books are equally suited to work with an individual pupil, and for use in Guided Reading sessions. The extra time allowed in Guided Reading sessions provides more opportunity to discuss the text and to fully explore comprehension.

Rapid Guided Reading Notes

This Teaching Guide provides easy-to-use Guided Reading notes for every text at *Rapid* Stages 1-3 (see pages 19-88). All the features of these notes are explained below.

Each text has a **lesson focus** linked to one of the following:

- *Speaking, Listening and Learning*, Primary National Strategy (DfES 0625-2003G)
- Target Statements for Reading (DfES).

This prepares pupils for the assessment questions at the end.

When you see this icon, you will find a **Speaking and Listening** objective.

A **synopsis** of the story or text gives you an overview of the read.

Suggestions for supporting children's reading are divided into three sections: **Before Reading**, **Strategy Check and Reading the Text** and **Responding to the Text**. See page 18 for detailed guidelines on structuring your Guided Reading session.

Assessing the Lesson Focus: Each Guided Reading session ends with an assessment based on the lesson focus. Involving children in assessment for learning helps them to focus on the task and to persevere for longer.

Linked photocopiable activity: A follow-up PCM has been provided for every text. These PCMs address either word-level skills or provide a writing task, and can be found in this Teaching Guide, directly after the Guided Reading notes for a particular book. The PCMs have been designed to be used independently by the pupils, who should be able to complete the tasks without adult supervision or further reference to the relevant book. You might like to use the PCMs directly after the Guided Reading session or for classwork / homework.

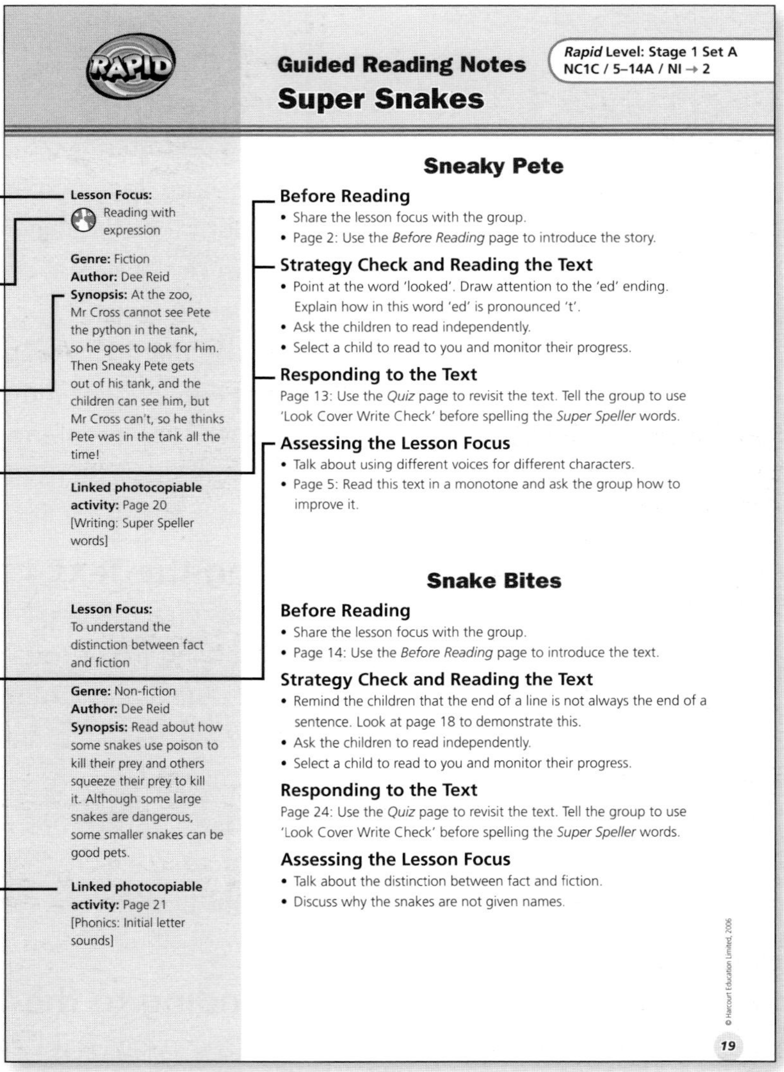

RAPID

Guided Reading Notes

Super Snakes

Rapid Level: Stage 1 Set A
NC1C / 5–14A / NI → 2

Sneaky Pete

Lesson Focus: Reading with expression

Genre: Fiction
Author: Dee Reid
Synopsis: At the zoo, Mr Cross cannot see Pete the python in the tank, so he goes to look for him. Then Sneaky Pete gets out of his tank, and the children can see him, but Mr Cross can't, so he thinks Pete was in the tank all the time!

Linked photocopiable activity: Page 20 [Writing: Super Speller words]

Before Reading
- Share the lesson focus with the group.
- Page 2: Use the *Before Reading* page to introduce the story.

Strategy Check and Reading the Text
- Point at the word 'looked'. Draw attention to the 'ed' ending. Explain how in this word 'ed' is pronounced 't'.
- Ask the children to read independently.
- Select a child to read to you and monitor their progress.

Responding to the Text
Page 13: Use the *Quiz* page to revisit the text. Tell the group to use 'Look Cover Write Check' before spelling the *Super Speller* words.

Assessing the Lesson Focus
- Talk about using different voices for different characters.
- Page 5: Read this text in a monotone and ask the group how to improve it.

Snake Bites

Lesson Focus: To understand the distinction between fact and fiction

Genre: Non-fiction
Author: Dee Reid
Synopsis: Read about how some snakes use poison to kill their prey and others squeeze their prey to kill it. Although some large snakes are dangerous, some smaller snakes can be good pets.

Linked photocopiable activity: Page 21 [Phonics: Initial letter sounds]

Before Reading
- Share the lesson focus with the group.
- Page 14: Use the *Before Reading* page to introduce the text.

Strategy Check and Reading the Text
- Remind the children that the end of a line is not always the end of a sentence. Look at page 18 to demonstrate this.
- Ask the children to read independently.
- Select a child to read to you and monitor their progress.

Responding to the Text
Page 24: Use the *Quiz* page to revisit the text. Tell the group to use 'Look Cover Write Check' before spelling the *Super Speller* words.

Assessing the Lesson Focus
- Talk about the distinction between fact and fiction.
- Discuss why the snakes are not given names.

19

The two texts within a *Rapid* Reading Book are provided with Guided Reading notes on the same page, allowing easy storage of the notes with the book. You may wish to photocopy the Guided Reading notes onto card, and keep this card alongside the relevant book.

Structuring your Guided Reading session with *Rapid*

1 **Introduce the Book and Select the Text**

2 **Share the Lesson Focus**

3 **Strategy Check**

Discuss with the group what to do if they come to a word they don't recognise. Encourage them to use a range of strategies, e.g. 'reading on', rereading', and 'sounding out'. Encourage pupils to self-correct if their reading is not making sense. A specific reading strategy is provided for each guided session, but teachers may wish to focus on a particular strategy that the group needs to practise.

4 **Before Reading**

This is the opportunity for the adult to set the scene for the readers. Use the *Before Reading* page to:

- talk about the characters and ensure that all the pupils can pronounce the names correctly (fiction texts); talk about the topic (non-fiction texts).
- introduce the 'Tricky words' and help the pupils to pronounce them. Ensure they understand the meaning of the words.
- read the Story/Text starter to the group. A number of the words and phrases that will be used in the text are previewed here to enable pupils to make a confident start when reading independently.

5 **Reading the Text**

During this time the pupils should read independently.

- Avoid asking pupils to take it in turn to read a page each as this reduces the amount of reading undertaken by any one pupil. Instead encourage 'simultaneous oral reading', when each pupil reads aloud quietly.
- Move around the group and 'tune in' to individual readers for a page or so to ensure that accurate reading is going on.
- Have quick word-level tasks for 'fast finishers', e.g. "Find a page with a question"; "Find a word which starts with a silent letter."

6 **Responding to the Text**

Use the *Quiz* page (Text Detective) to monitor how well the pupils have understood what they have read.

- Invite the pupils to share their reflections upon the text.
- Encourage them to listen to one another and to build upon one another's responses.

7 **Assessing the Lesson Focus**

This is the opportunity to revisit the focus introduced at the start of the session.

Super Snakes

Rapid Level: Stage 1 Set A
NC1C / 5–14A / NI → 2

Sneaky Pete

Lesson Focus:
 Reading with expression

Genre: Fiction
Author: Dee Reid
Synopsis: At the zoo, Mr Cross cannot see Pete the python in the tank, so he goes to look for him. Then Sneaky Pete gets out of his tank, and the children can see him, but Mr Cross can't, so he thinks Pete was in the tank all the time!

Linked photocopiable activity: Page 20 [Writing: Super Speller words]

Before Reading

- Share the lesson focus with the group.
- Page 2: Use the *Before Reading* page to introduce the story.

Strategy Check and Reading the Text

- Point at the word 'looked'. Draw attention to the 'ed' ending. Explain how in this word 'ed' is pronounced 't'.
- Ask the children to read independently.
- Select a child to read to you and monitor their progress.

Responding to the Text

Page 13: Use the *Quiz* page to revisit the text. Tell the group to use 'Look Cover Write Check' before spelling the *Super Speller* words.

Assessing the Lesson Focus

- Talk about using different voices for different characters.
- Page 5: Read this text in a monotone and ask the group how to improve it.

Snake Bites

Lesson Focus:
To understand the distinction between fact and fiction

Genre: Non-fiction
Author: Dee Reid
Synopsis: Read about how some snakes use poison to kill their prey and others squeeze their prey to kill it. Although some large snakes are dangerous, some smaller snakes can be good pets.

Linked photocopiable activity: Page 21 [Phonics: Initial letter sounds]

Before Reading

- Share the lesson focus with the group.
- Page 14: Use the *Before Reading* page to introduce the text.

Strategy Check and Reading the Text

- Remind the children that the end of a line is not always the end of a sentence. Look at page 18 to demonstrate this.
- Ask the children to read independently.
- Select a child to read to you and monitor their progress.

Responding to the Text

Page 24: Use the *Quiz* page to revisit the text. Tell the group to use 'Look Cover Write Check' before spelling the *Super Speller* words.

Assessing the Lesson Focus

- Talk about the distinction between fact and fiction.
- Discuss why the snakes are not given names.

Name: ______________________ Date: ____________

Sneaky Pete

Write over the word ‘see’ in blue.
Write over the word ‘but’ in red.
Write over the word ‘to’ in green.

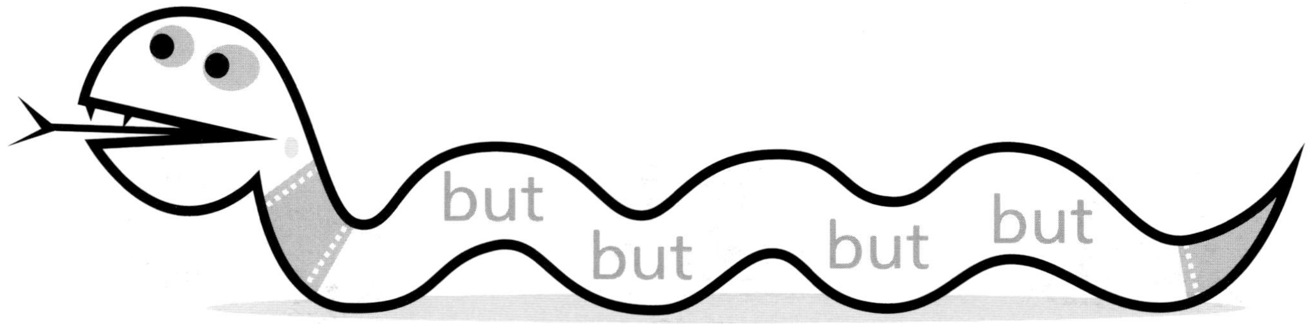

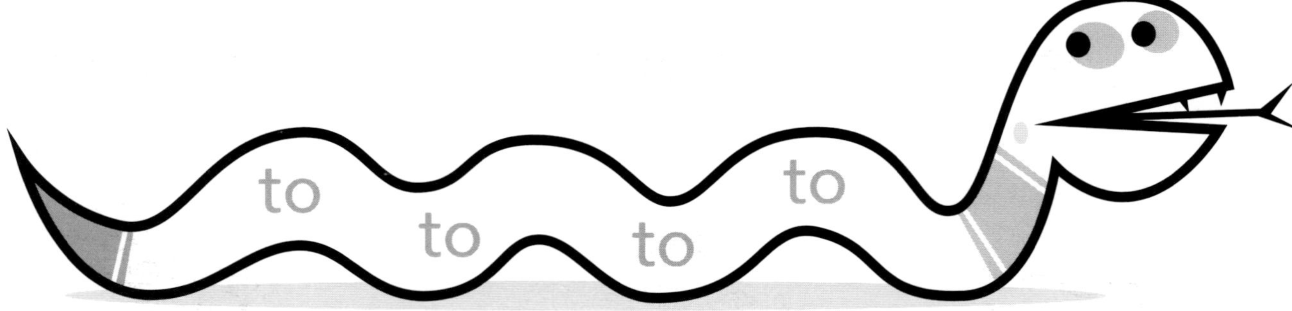

Now write the words.

__________ __________ __________

Name: ______________________ Date: ____________

Snake Bites

Circle the correct letter, then write it to complete the word.

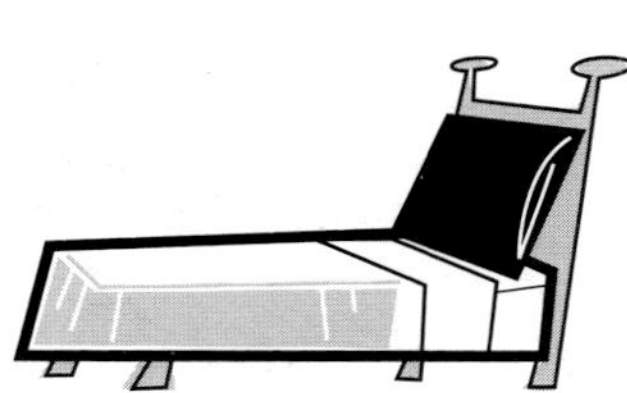

b p

__ed

r d

__og

c m

__at

l h

__at

f t

__elevision

s k

__kateboard

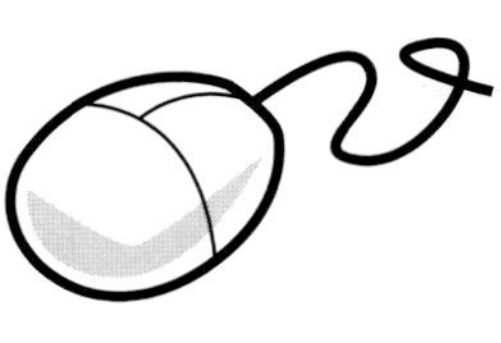

m n

__ouse

n m

__est

r w

__atch

Guided Reading Notes
Trunk Tales

Rapid Level: Stage 1 Set A
NC1C / 5–14A / NI → 2

Naughty Nellie

Lesson Focus:
Making predictions

Genre: Fiction
Author: Dee Reid
Synopsis: At the zoo, Mr Cross is squirted with water. He tries to find out who did it – he thinks it was Nellie, the elephant. But the children say it was not Nellie because she is good. Then Nellie squirts water over the children!

Linked photocopiable activity: Page 23 [Writing: Super Speller words]

Before Reading
- Share the lesson focus with the group. Ask them to predict what naughty things Nellie will do.
- Page 2: Use the *Before Reading* page to introduce the story.

Strategy Check and Reading the Text
- Demonstrate blending phonemes, e.g. page 4 'd-i-d'.
- Ask the children to read independently.
- Select a child to read to you and monitor their progress.

Responding to the Text
Page13: Use the *Quiz* page to revisit the text. Tell the group to use 'Look Cover Write Check' before spelling the *Super Speller words*.

Assessing the Lesson Focus
- Ask the children if their predictions were correct.
- Page 3: What is the clue that Nellie squirted water at Mr Cross?
- Page 12: What do the children think will happen next?

Elephants

Lesson Focus:
To acquire new words from reading

Genre: Non-fiction
Author: Dee Reid
Synopsis: Read about elephants, their huge size and the many things they can do with their long trunks.

Linked photocopiable activity: Page 24 [Phonics: Initial letter sounds]

Before Reading
- Share the lesson focus with the group.
- Page 14: Use the *Before Reading* page to introduce the text.

Strategy Check and Reading the Text
- Encourage the children to tackle unfamiliar words by blending phonemes to read, e.g. 'man' and 'van' (page 16).
- Ask the children to read independently.
- Select a child to read to you and monitor their progress.

Responding to the Text
Page 24: Use the *Quiz* page to revisit the text. Tell the group to use 'Look Cover Write Check' before spelling the *Super Speller words*.

Assessing the Lesson Focus
- Talk about the words 'trunk' and 'bull'. Explain that these are technical words for non-fiction texts.
- What is the most interesting fact the children have learned?

Name: ______________________ Date: ____________

Naughty Nellie

Write over these words.

did the at no me

Now use the words to make the sentences.

"Who squirted water ____ me?" said Mr Cross.

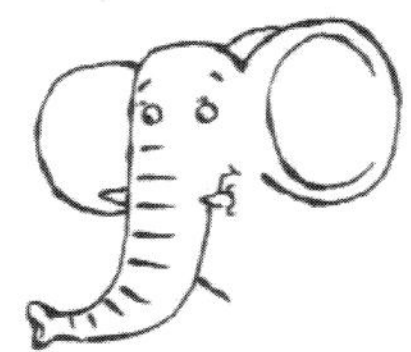

"Not ____ ," said Nellie.

"Oh yes, you _____ ," said Mr Cross.

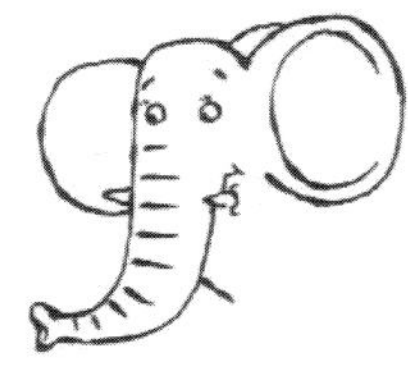

Nellie squirted water all over ____ children.

"Oh ____!!!" said the children.

Name: ______________________ Date: ______________

Elephants

Write over these letters.

Add the letters to make the words.

____is ____an ____e ____ey ____at

Now write the words.

________ ________ ________ ________ ________

Guided Reading Notes
Chimps and Us

Rapid Level: Stage 1 Set A
NC1C / 5–14A / NI → 2

Are You Like a Chimpanzee?

Lesson Focus:
 Answering questions

Genre: Non-fiction
Author: Dee Reid
Synopsis: In some ways chimpanzees are like humans. Chimpanzees laugh, hug and kiss, but there are some important differences: chimpanzees walk on all fours and pick fleas off each other!

Linked photocopiable activity: Page 26 [Phonics: Initial letter sounds]

Before Reading

- Share the lesson focus with the group.
- Page 2: Use the *Before Reading* page to introduce the text.

Strategy Check and Reading the Text

- Demonstrate syllabification, e.g. page 3: break the word 'chimpanzee' into three syllables: chim/pan/zee.
- Ask the children to read independently.
- Select a child to read to you and monitor their progress.

Responding to the Text

Page 11: Use the *Quiz* page to revisit the text. Tell the group to use 'Look Cover Write Check' before spelling the *Super Speller* words.

Assessing the Lesson Focus

- Page 3: Ask individual children to read the question on this page. How do they know it is a question? How should it be read?
- Page 8: Point to the question "Do you?" Ask the children what it refers to. Discuss answers to this and the question on page 9.

Cheeky Charlie

Lesson Focus:
 To read with expression

Genre: Fiction
Author: Dee Reid
Synopsis: At the zoo, Cheeky Charlie the chimpanzee takes Mr Cross's cap. First he puts it on his head, then he sits on it. Mr Cross doesn't know where his cap has gone. Then Charlie drops the cap back on Mr Cross's head!

Linked photocopiable activity: Page 27 [Writing: Super speller words]

Before Reading

- Share the lesson focus with the group.
- Page 12: Use the *Before Reading* page to introduce the story.

Strategy Check and Reading the Text

- Demonstrate blending phonemes, e.g. blend the phonemes to read the words 'c-a-p' (page 13) and 's-a-t' (page 16).
- Ask the children to read independently.
- Select a child to read to you and monitor their progress.

Responding to the Text

Page 24: Use the *Quiz* page to revisit the text. Tell the group to use 'Look Cover Write Check' before spelling the *Super Speller words.*

Assessing the Lesson Focus

- Read the story as a play, with you taking the part of Mr Cross.
- Ask the children to read the words of the children. Encourage them to read with expression.

Name: ______________________ Date: ____________

Are You Like a Chimpanzee?

Write over the first letter, then join the word to the picture.

hand

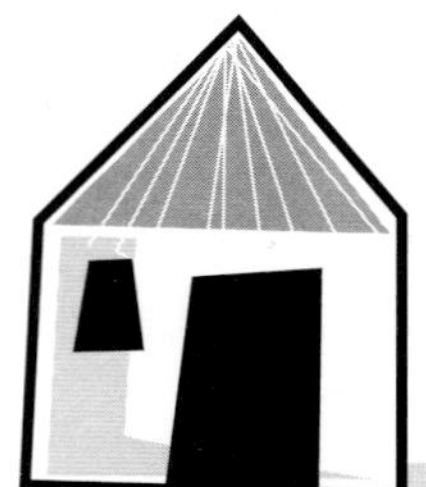

hill

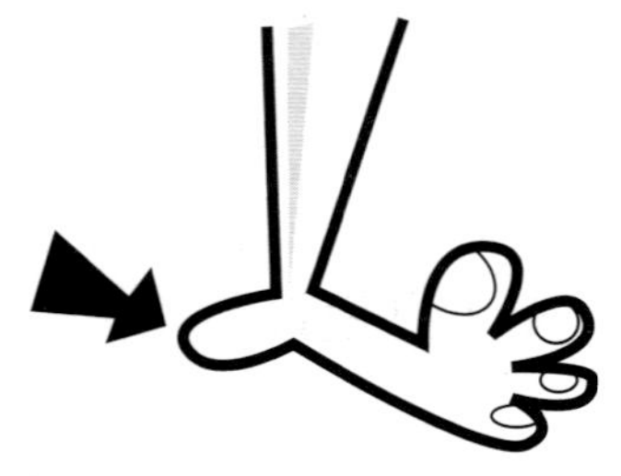

hat

hut

hen

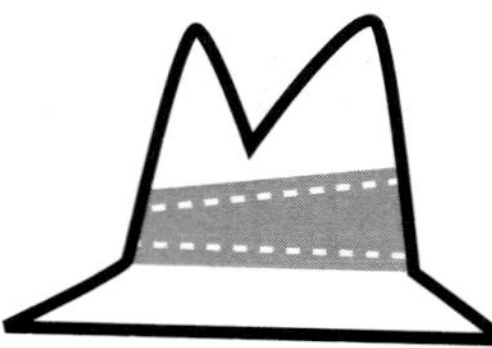

heel

Which endings need 'h' to make a word?

___ad   ___is   ___om   ___er   ___ow   ___id

Name: ______________________________ Date: ______________

Cheeky Charlie

Choose the word to go in the sentence.

my is on

"Where is _____ cap?" said Mr Cross.

---

is my on

Charlie put the cap _____ his head.

---

is my on

"Give me back _____ cap," said Mr Cross.

---

is my on

Charlie sat _____ the cap.

---

is my on

"Where _____ my cap?" said Mr Cross.

---

is my on

"Charlie ____ on it," said the children.

Big Cats, Small Cats

Are Lions like Cats?

Lesson Focus:

 Using intonation when asking a question

Genre: Non-fiction
Author: Dee Reid
Synopsis: In some ways lions and cats are similar. They are both good at hunting and they both like climbing. But male lions have manes, and lions live together in a pride, so there are differences too.

Linked photocopiable activity: Page 29
[Phonics: Initial letter sounds]

Before Reading

- Share the lesson focus with the group.
- Page 2: Use the *Before Reading* page to introduce the text.

Strategy Check and Reading the Text

- Demonstrate syllabification by splitting the words 'hunting' (page 3) and 'climbing' (page 4) into syllables: hunt/ing; climb/ing.
- Ask the children to read independently.
- Select a child to read to you and monitor their progress.

Responding to the Text

Page 11: Use the *Quiz* page to revisit the text. Tell the group to use 'Look Cover Write Check' before spelling the *Super Speller* words.

Assessing the Lesson Focus

- Page 3: Ask individual children to read the question on this page. How do they know it is a question? How should it be read?
- Page 9: In pairs, one child reads the statement and the other reads the question. What sounds different?

Lazy Leo

Lesson Focus:

 To read with expression

Genre: Fiction
Author: Dee Reid
Synopsis: At the zoo, Mr Cross and the children find Leo the lion asleep. The children think he is boring. But when Leo wakes up and roars, Mr Cross and the children think they might prefer it when he is asleep!

Linked photocopiable activity: Page 30
[Writing: Linking speech bubbles to characters]

Before Reading

- Share the lesson focus with the group.
- Page 12: Use the *Before Reading* page to introduce the story.

Strategy Check and Reading the Text

- Demonstrate how to look carefully at small differences between words, e.g. page 13 'wake' and page 16 'woke'.
- Ask the children to read independently.
- Select a child to read to you and monitor their progress.

Responding to the Text

Page 24: Use the *Quiz* page to revisit the text. Tell the group to use 'Look Cover Write Check' before spelling the *Super Speller* words.

Assessing the Lesson Focus

- Page 20: Ask the children why the word 'roared' is written differently. Ask individual children to demonstrate how it should be read.

Name: ______________________________ Date: ______________

Are Lions like Cats?

Draw a line from each object to the animal that starts with the same letter.

l

c

Write ‘l’ or ‘c’ to make some words.

__an __ip __ut __eg __et __at

Name: ______________________________ Date: ______________

Lazy Leo

Who said what?
Join each speech bubble to the right character.

Stop!

I will be a good lion.

You can't sleep all day.

Go away!

Write over the words in the speech bubble.

Can I sleep now?

PCM WRITING

Chocolate Chunks

Lesson Focus:

To use intonation when reading

Genre: Fiction
Author: Alison Hawes
Synopsis: Tim and the Pest go to get some milk from the shop. The Pest wants some chocolates and puts them in the basket. Tim and the Pest begin to fight, but the Pest sees a robber taking some chocolate and lets go. Tim falls into a pile of tins and one of them hits the robber.

Linked photocopiable activity: Page 32
[Writing: True or False?]

Tim, the Pest and the Chocolate Robber

Before Reading

- Share the lesson focus with the group.
- Page 2: Use the *Before Reading* page to introduce the story.

Strategy Check and Reading the Text

- Encourage the children to tackle unfamiliar words by rereading the text to check for sense.
- Ask the children to read independently.
- Select a child to read to you and monitor their progress.

Responding to the Text

Page 13: Use the *Quiz* page to revisit the text. Tell the group to use 'Look Cover Write Check' before spelling the *Super Speller* words.

Assessing the Lesson Focus

- Ask individual children to read selected pages to the group. Talk about putting in expression and emphasis.
- Page 9: Ask why the word 'OW!' is written in bold.

Lesson Focus:

To take turns to speak and listen to others

Genre: Non-fiction
Author: Alison Hawes
Synopsis: Chocolate does not always come in bars. People eat chocolate with different foods, and in different countries.

Linked photocopiable activity: Page 33
[Phonics: Final letter sounds]

Chocolate World

Before Reading

- Share the lesson focus with the group.
- Page 14: Use the *Before Reading* page to introduce the text.

Strategy Check and Reading the Text

- Encourage the children to tackle an unfamiliar word by breaking the words into syllables, e.g. page 15 'choc/o/late'.
- Ask the children to read independently.
- Select a child to read to you and monitor their progress.

Responding to the Text

Page 24: Use the *Quiz* page to revisit the text. Tell the group to use 'Look Cover Write Check' before spelling the *Super Speller words*.

Assessing the Lesson Focus

- Ask the group what new facts they have learned about chocolate. Encourage them to take turns answering and listening to each other.

Name: ______________________________ Date: ______________

Tim, the Pest and the Chocolate Robber

Circle the right answer.

Tim put the milk in the basket.

True False

Tim put the chocolates in the basket.

True False

"Put the chocolates back!" said Tim.

True False

"He is a milk robber!" said the Pest.

True False

A tin fell on the chocolate robber.

True False

Tim and the Pest got some chocolates.

True False

Name: ______________________ Date: ____________

Chocolate World

Choose a final sound (letter) to make new words. The first ones have been done for you.

Look out – there's one letter you can't use!

bi_	t bit	b bib	d bid	m ____	n bin
bu_	d ____	g ____	b ____	n ____	s ____
ma_	n ____	b ____	p ____	t ____	d ____
ro_	b ____	g ____	d ____	t ____	ck ____

PCM PHONICS

Guided Reading Notes
Daring Dogs

Rapid Level: Stage 1 Set B
NC1C / 5–14A / NI → 2

Dogs to the Rescue

Lesson Focus:

 To answer questions about the text

Genre: Non-fiction
Author: Alison Hawes
Synopsis: Rescue dogs are used in many different situations. They help people buried in deep snow, people lost on mountains, and even people trapped in collapsed buildings.

Linked photocopiable activity: Page 35 [Phonics: Final letter sounds]

Before Reading
- Share the lesson focus with the group.
- Page 2: Use the *Before Reading* page to introduce the text.

Strategy Check and Reading the Text
- Encourage the children to tackle unfamiliar words by rereading the text to check for sense.
- Ask the children to read independently.
- Select a child to read to you and monitor their progress.

Responding to the Text
Page 11: Use the *Quiz* page to revisit the text. Tell the group to use 'Look Cover Write Check' before spelling the *Super Speller* words.

Assessing the Lesson Focus
Ask the children to find the answers to the following questions:
- How do dogs find people trapped in deep snow?
- How do they tell the rescue team where to go?
- How do dogs find people trapped in collapsed buildings?

Tim, the Pest and the Big Dog

Lesson Focus:

 To re-tell a simple story

Genre: Fiction
Author: Alison Hawes
Synopsis: Tim and Buster want to go to the park but the Pest wants to go too. She really wants to hold Buster's lead. Then Buster runs off and jumps into a pond. Tim finally gives the Pest Buster's lead to hold and Buster shakes water all over the Pest!

Linked photocopiable activity: Page 36 [Writing: High-frequency words]

Before Reading
- Share the lesson focus with the group.
- Page 12: Use the *Before Reading* page to introduce the story.

Strategy Check and Reading the Text
- Encourage the children to read ahead to discover what an unfamiliar word might mean.
- Ask the children to read independently.
- Select a child to read to you and monitor their progress.

Responding to the Text
Page 24: Use the *Quiz* page to revisit the text. Tell the group to use 'Look Cover Write Check' before spelling the *Super Speller* words.

Assessing the Lesson Focus
- Ask the children to re-tell the story. Ask them what happened at the start when Tim and the Pest got to the park, and at the end of the story.
- Discuss whether the ending is funny – or do the children think that Tim is unkind?

Name: ________________ Date: ________

Dogs to the Rescue

Use these letters to make six words ending in 'g'.

a b d e g i l m o p

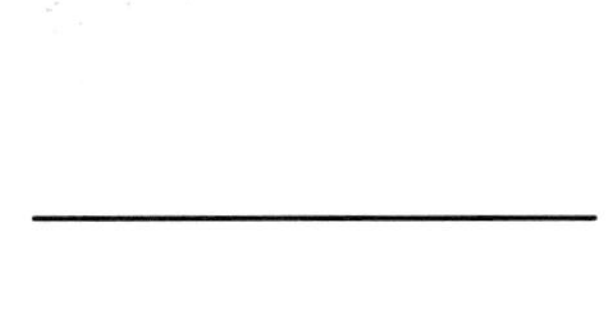

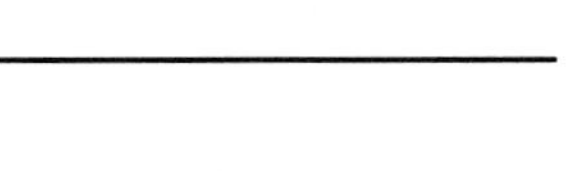

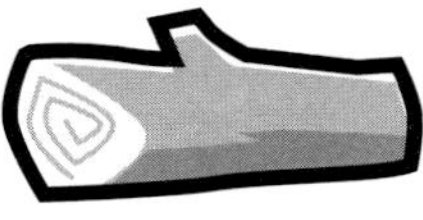

Name: ______________________ Date: ______________

Tim, the Pest and the Big Dog

Circle the word 'pull'. Can you find 10?

pull	put	play	pull	full	put
ball	pull	play	pull	call	bell
pull	pull	put	pill	pull	full
ball	pull	bull	dull	pull	pull

Now write the word.

pull ____________ ____________ ____________

Buster will __________ the Pest.

Guided Reading Notes

Rapid Level: Stage 1 Set B
NC1C / 5–14A / NI → 2

Monsters!

Lesson Focus:
To predict when reading

Genre: Fiction
Author: Alison Hawes
Synopsis: Tim wants to see a film about monsters, but he has to take the Pest with him. Big Biffo laughs at Tim. In the film, an ice monster puts his hands on a boy's neck. The Pest gets the last laugh when she scares Big Biffo by putting an ice lolly on his neck.

Linked photocopiable activity: Page 38 [Writing: Sequencing sentences]

Tim, the Pest and the Ice Monster

Before Reading

- Share the lesson focus with the group.
- Page 2: Use the *Before Reading* page to introduce the story.

Strategy Check and Reading the Text

- Encourage the children to tackle unfamiliar words by rereading the text to check for sense.
- Ask the children to read independently.
- Select a child to read to you and monitor their progress.

Responding to the Text

Page 13: Use the *Quiz* page to revisit the text. Tell the group to use 'Look Cover Write Check' before spelling the *Super Speller* words.

Assessing the Lesson Focus

- Ask the children if anyone guessed what would happen to Big Biffo. What clues were there that helped them to guess?
- Ask the children if they have ever been scared watching a film.

Lesson Focus:
 To take turns to speak and to listen to others

Genre: Non-fiction
Author: Alison Hawes
Synopsis: Monsters in films look scary, but they are made to look scary in different ways: sometimes they are just models, sometimes it is done with make-up, and sometimes it is done using a computer picture.

Linked photocopiable activity: Page 39 [Phonics: Final letter sounds]

Monsters on Film

Before Reading

- Share the lesson focus with the group.
- Page14: Use the *Before Reading* page to introduce the text.

Strategy Check and Reading the Text

- Encourage the children to tackle unfamiliar words by breaking longer words into syllables, e.g. page 17 'Frank/en/stein'.
- Ask the children to read independently.
- Select a child to read to you and monitor their progress.

Responding to the Text

Page 24: Use the *Quiz* page to revisit the text. Tell the group to use 'Look Cover Write Check' before spelling the *Super Speller* words.

Assessing the Lesson Focus

- Ask the group to take it in turns to say which monster they thought was the most scary. They should listen to each other's choices and then vote on which monster was the most scary.

Name: ______________________ Date: ____________

Tim, the Pest and the Ice Monster

Put the sentences in the right order.

Tim wanted to see a film.

The Pest wanted an ice lolly.

Big Biffo laughed at Tim.

The Pest put her ice lolly on Big Biffo's neck.

The Ice Monster put his ice hands on a boy's neck.

The Pest wanted to see the film, too.

Name: ______________________ Date: ____________

Monsters on Film

Circle the correct letter, then write it to complete the word.

n p

su___

b g

do___

t m

ca___

p s

bu___

k l

boo___

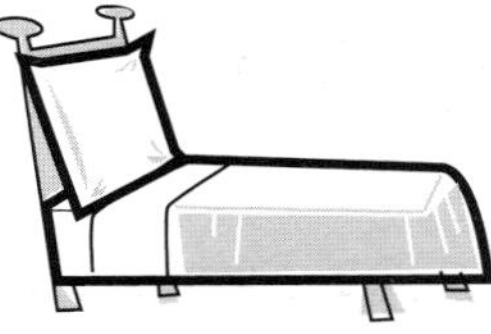

l d

be___

p d

zi___

p b

bi___

m n

ja___

Sports Mad

Lesson Focus:

To ask and answer questions

Genre: Non-fiction
Author: Alison Hawes
Synopsis: Crazy things can happen in sports. A referee once sent off an entire rugby team, a dog scored a goal in a football match and even a butterfly once helped a golfer to put a ball in the hole!

Linked photocopiable activity: Page 41
[Phonics: Final letter sounds]

Match Crazy

Before Reading

- Share the lesson focus with the group.
- Page 2: Use the *Before Reading* page to introduce the text.

Strategy Check and Reading the Text

- Encourage the children to self-correct errors by rereading the text to reinforce understanding.
- Ask the children to read independently.
- Select a child to read to you and monitor their progress.

Responding to the Text

Page 11: Use the *Quiz* page to revisit the text. Tell the group to use 'Look Cover Write Check' before spelling the *Super Speller* words.

Assessing the Lesson Focus

- Demonstrate how to ask questions. For example, "How many players did the referee send off in the rugby match?"
- Ask the children to work with a partner and allocate different sports to each pair. Tell them to work out a question for their sport. The other children should try to answer their questions.

Lesson Focus:

To interpret a text by reading aloud with pace and emphasis

Genre: Fiction
Author: Alison Hawes
Synopsis: Tim and the Pest go to a football match on a windy day. When the Pest's new cap blows on to the pitch, she runs after it, and Tim runs after the Pest! Tim then crashes straight into a footballer!

Linked photocopiable activity: Page 42
[Writing: High-frequency words]

Tim, the Pest and the Footballer

Before Reading

- Share the lesson focus with the group.
- Page 2: Use the *Before Reading* page to introduce the story.

Strategy Check and Reading the Text

- Encourage the children to tackle unfamiliar words by looking for known words within other words, e.g. page 4 'foot-ball'.
- Ask the children to read independently.
- Select a child to read to you and monitor their progress.

Responding to the Text

Page 24: Use the *Quiz* page to revisit the text. Tell the group to use 'Look Cover Write Check' before spelling the *Super Speller* words.

Assessing the Lesson Focus

- Ask the children if they know what speech marks are for.
- Ask three children to take the parts of Tim, the Pest and the footballer, and to read with intonation and expression.
- Repeat with the other members of the group.

Name: ______________________ Date: ____________

Match Crazy

Write over the letters.

Then use a letter to make some words.

t d g n p

The first one has been done for you.

co	cod	cog	cot
ba	______	______	______
di	______	______	______
pe	______	______	______

PCM PHONICS

Name: ______________________________ Date: ____________

Tim, the Pest and the Footballer

Study the word, then fold the paper to cover it. Write the word, check it, then write the word again – fast!

Look	Cover	Write	Check ✔ or ✘	Write fast
the		________		________
sent		________		________
off		________		________
one		________		________
into		________		________
hit		________		________
ate		________		________
ball		________		________

Fold

Pedal Power

Lesson Focus:
To deduce what might happen in a text

Genre: Fiction
Author: Jeremy Taylor
Synopsis: Tom is travelling too fast on his bike. He hits a hole in the road and, luckily, he flies over the hedge, the nettles, a haystack, and a pitchfork! But then his luck runs out and he lands in a pool of mud.

Linked photocopiable activity: Page 44
[Writing: Completing sentences]

On Your Bike!

Before Reading

- Share the lesson focus with the group.
- Page 2: Use the *Before Reading* page to introduce the story.

Strategy Check and Reading the Text

- Encourage the children to tackle unfamiliar words by rereading the text to check for sense.
- Ask the children to read independently.
- Select a child to read to you and monitor their progress.

Responding to the Text

Page 13: Use the *Quiz* page to revisit the text. Tell the group to use 'Look Cover Write Check' before spelling the *Super Speller* words.

Assessing the Lesson Focus

- Look at the illustrations and ask the group how these would tell them that Tom was not very happy.
- Stopping at each page, work through the text, asking the group what they thought might happen to Tom. What actually happened?

Lesson Focus:
 To locate specific information in a text to find answers to simple questions

Genre: Non-fiction
Author: Jeremy Taylor
Synopsis: Riding bikes is good fun, but it can be dangerous. Some people like mountain-bike racing, some like speed racing, some ride around the world, and some people enter the world's biggest bike race .

Linked photocopiable activity: Page 45
[Phonics: Making CVC words]

All Kinds of Bikes

Before Reading

- Share the lesson focus with the group.
- Page 14: Use the *Before Reading* page to introduce the text.

Strategy Check and Reading the Text

- Encourage the children to tackle unfamiliar words by breaking the word into syllables, e.g. page 16 'dan/ger/ous'.
- Ask the children to read independently.
- Select a child to read to you and monitor their progress.

Responding to the Text

Page 24: Use the *Quiz* page to revisit the text. Tell the group to use 'Look Cover Write Check' before spelling the *Super Speller* words.

Assessing the Lesson Focus

Ask the group simple questions about the different bike rides:

- Page 17: Where is this man riding his bike?
  Which word gives them the answer? (mountain)
- Page 18: What do speed-bike racers have to wear? (helmets)

Name: ______________________ Date: ____________

On Your Bike!

Complete the sentences using the words from the box below.

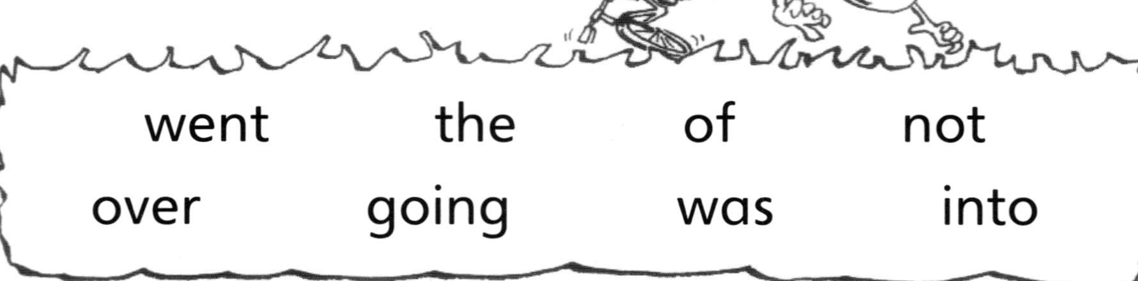

went	the	of	not
over	going	was	into

Tom __________ on his bike.

He was __________ into a hedge.

He flew __________ the hedge.

He was going __________ the nettles.

But he did __________ go into the nettles.

He __________ over the haystack.

But he went into ________ pool ________ mud.

Name: ______________________ Date: ____________

All Kinds of Bikes

Add a consonant to make a word.

b	d	f	h	m	n	p	s

Make three-letter words using these letters.

All the words have 'o' in the middle.

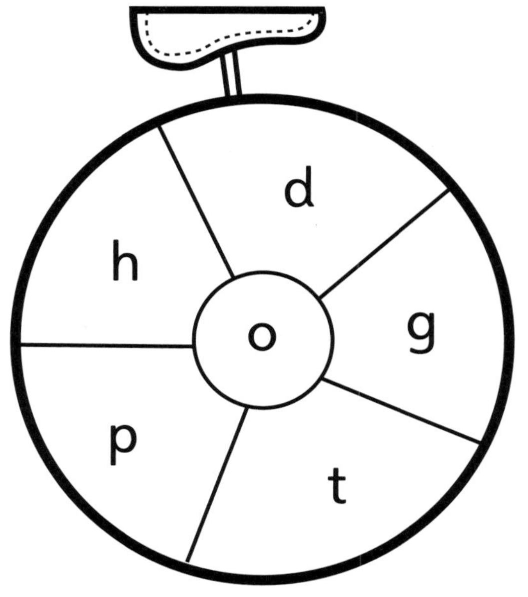

____________ ____________

____________ ____________

____________ ____________

Guided Reading Notes

Just the Job!

Rapid Level: Stage 2 Set A
NC1B / 5–14A / NI → 2

Lesson Focus:

 To explain or give reasons for their views

Genre: Non-fiction
Author: Jeremy Taylor
Synopsis: Some people have crazy jobs. Some jobs are boring, like checking carrots or putting letters in envelopes. Others are very exciting, like looking after crocodiles, working on TV, or being a referee at a football match!

Linked photocopiable activity: Page 47
[Phonics: Matching rhyming words]

Crazy Jobs

Before Reading

- Share the lesson focus with the group.
- Page 2: Use the *Before Reading* page to introduce the text.

Strategy Check and Reading the Text

- Encourage the children to tackle unfamiliar words by breaking the word into syllables, e.g. page 3 'choc/o/late'.
- Ask the children to read independently.
- Select a child to read to you and monitor their progress.

Responding to the Text

Page 11: Use the *Quiz* page to revisit the text. Tell the group to use 'Look Cover Write Check' before spelling the *Super Speller* words.

Assessing the Lesson Focus

- Ask the children which they think is the most boring job and the most exciting, giving reasons for their choice.
- Ask the children what jobs would they like to have and why.

Lesson Focus:

 To sequence events in a story

Genre: Fiction
Author: Jeremy Taylor
Synopsis: Tom sees a cool bike that he really wants, but he cannot afford it. He works hard for his family, and earns some money, but it is not enough for the bike. But it is enough for some cool rollerblades instead.

Linked photocopiable activity: Page 48
[Writing: High-frequency words]

I Want a New Bike!

Before Reading

- Share the lesson focus with the group.
- Page 12: Use the *Before Reading* page to introduce the story.

Strategy Check and Reading the Text

- Encourage the children to self-correct errors by rereading the sentence to reinforce understanding.
- Ask the children to read independently.
- Select a child to read to you and monitor their progress.

Responding to the Text

Page 24: Use the *Quiz* page to revisit the text. Tell the group to use 'Look Cover Write Check' before spelling the *Super Speller* words.

Assessing the Lesson Focus

- Ask the children to work with a partner and to discuss the sequence of events in the story.
- When they are ready, ask them to tell the events of the story in order.

Name: ______________________________ Date:

Crazy Jobs

Change the first letter to make a new rhyming word.

will ★ hill get ★ ______ top ★ ______

pot ★ ______ bat ★ ______

can ★ ______ bit ★ ______ fun ★ ______

had ★ ______ man ★ ______

pen ★ ______ met ★ ______ hid ★ ______

Name: ______________________ Date: ____________

I Want a New Bike!

Circle the word 'want'. Can you find 10?

want	went	will	want	what	warm
want	went	tent	want	what	want
warm	welt	want	want	bent	mend
want	warm	wart	when	why	want
sent	want	wear	went	wand	wasp

Now write the word.

want ________ ________ ________

I ________ a new bike.

I ______ to help you.

I ______ some rollerblades.

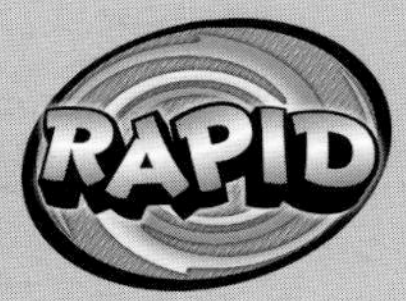

Guided Reading Notes

Do You Believe It?

Real Snowmen

Lesson Focus:

To explain or give reasons for their views

Genre: Non-fiction
Author: Jeremy Taylor
Synopsis: Many people make snowmen out of snow, but in Nepal people say there are real snowmen. They are called Yeti and people say they have seen their footprints. Do Yeti really exist?

Linked photocopiable activity: Page 50 [Phonics: Making three-letter words]

Before Reading

- Share the lesson focus with the group.
- Page 2: Use the *Before Reading* page to introduce the text.

Strategy Check and Reading the Text

- Encourage the children to tackle unfamiliar words by looking for known words within words, e.g. page 5 'snow-men'.
- Ask the children to read independently.
- Select a child to read to you and monitor their progress.

Responding to the Text

Page 11: Use the *Quiz* page to revisit the text. Tell the group to use 'Look Cover Write Check' before spelling the *Super Speller* words.

Assessing the Lesson Focus

Discuss with the group the evidence for whether the Yeti exists or not:

- Look at pages 6 and 7. Ask the children whether they think this picture is a photograph or not. Ask them for their reasons.
- Look at page 9. Ask the children whether this photograph is enough to prove that the Yeti exists.

The Old Skateboard

Lesson Focus:

To take turns to speak and listen to others

Genre: Fiction
Author: Jeremy Taylor
Synopsis: Tom has an old skateboard. One snowy day he is skating and the wheels come off – one by one! He solves the problem by turning his skateboard into a snowboard.

Linked photocopiable activity: Page 51 [Writing: Look, Cover, Write, Check]

Before Reading

- Share the lesson focus with the group.
- Page 12: Use the *Before Reading* page to introduce the story.

Strategy Check and Reading the Text

- Encourage the children to read ahead in the text to discover what an unfamiliar word might be.
- Ask the children to read independently.
- Select a child to read to you and monitor their progress.

Responding to the Text

Page 24: Use the *Quiz* page to revisit the text. Tell the group to use 'Look Cover Write Check' before spelling the *Super Speller words*.

Assessing the Lesson Focus

- Ask the group to re-tell the story taking it in turns to say what happened.
- Ask the group to say if the speaker has included everything. Have they remembered what happened to Tom's skateboard and what Kim said each time?

Name: ______________________ Date: ____________

Real Snowmen

Make words in the Yeti footprints.

b c d f g h j k l m n p r s t v w

The first one is done for you.

m a n

_ a _

_ e _

_ e _

_ e _

_ i _

_ i _

_ i _

_ o _

_ o _

_ o _

_ u _

_ u _

_ u _

PCM PHONICS

Name: ______________________ Date: ____________

The Old Skateboard

Study the word, then fold the paper to cover it. Write the word, check it, then write the word again – fast!

Look	Fold	Cover	Write	Check ✔ or ✘	Write fast
was			________		________
has			________		________
stop			________		________
now			________		________
come			________		________
with			________		________
have			________		________
had			________		________

PCM WRITING

Guided Reading Notes

Don't Drop It!

Rapid Level: Stage 2 Set A
NC1B / 5–14A / NI → 2

Star-struck Tom

Lesson Focus:

To use intonation when reading

Genre: Fiction
Author: Jeremy Taylor
Synopsis: Tom sees a tennis star on the TV and decides to become a tennis star himself. He practises hard but his racket is very old. So Tom decides to use his tennis balls to become a juggling star. When a TV man sees Tom juggling, he asks him to juggle on TV.

Linked photocopiable activity: Page 53 [Writing: Re-ordering words in sentences]

Before Reading

- Share the lesson focus with the group.
- Page 2: Use the *Before Reading* page to introduce the story.

Strategy Check and Reading the Text

- Encourage the children to self-correct errors by returning to the start of the sentence.
- Ask the children to read independently.
- Select a child to read to you and monitor their progress.

Responding to the Text

Page 13: Use the *Quiz* page to revisit the text. Tell the group to use 'Look Cover Write Check' before spelling the *Super Speller* words.

Assessing the Lesson Focus

- Read pages 3 and 4 to the group with expression, pace and intonation.
- Ask individual children to read selected pages and discuss how to make the reading more interesting by using intonation and pace. The other members of the group should evaluate the reading.

How to Juggle

Lesson Focus:

To read with expression

Genre: Non-fiction
Author: Jeremy Taylor
Synopsis: Juggling means keeping several balls in the air at the same time. You have to practise how to pass the balls from one hand to the other hand, and back again. Some people can juggle with fire, some can juggle while walking on stilts and some can even juggle with tables!

Linked photocopiable activity: Page 54 [Phonics: Making CVC words]

Before Reading

- Have some juggling balls or bags for the group to try.
- Share the lesson focus with the group.
- Page 14: Use the *Before Reading* page to introduce the text.

Strategy Check and Reading the Text

- Encourage the children to break up unfamiliar words into syllables, e.g. page 15 'jugg/ling', and page 20 'ba/na/nas'.
- Ask the children to read independently.
- Select a child to read to you and monitor their progress.

Responding to the Text

Page 24: Use the *Quiz* page to revisit the text. Tell the group to use 'Look Cover Write Check' before spelling the *Super Speller* words.

Assessing the Lesson Focus

- Give two children three juggling balls each. Ask another to read the instructions on pages 15-17 for the jugglers to try to follow. Another child reads pages 18-19.
- Repeat, using different children to be the jugglers and the readers.

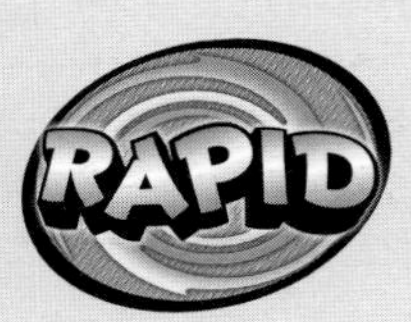

Name: ______________________ Date: ____________

Star-struck Tom

Sort out the muddled sentences.

Don't forget the full stops!

Tom said, "big be star a I can."

Tom said, " ______________________ "

Tom said, "I on TV can be."

Tom said, " ______________________ "

Tom said, "juggling I be can star a."

Tom said, " ______________________ "

So was Tom TV on.

So ______________________

Kim said, "are You a star juggling."

Kim said, " ______________________ "

PCM WRITING

Name: ______________________ Date: ____________

How to Juggle

Make three-letter words.

d	b	c	g	h	k	l
f	m	p	r	s	t	

Use the letters in the box.

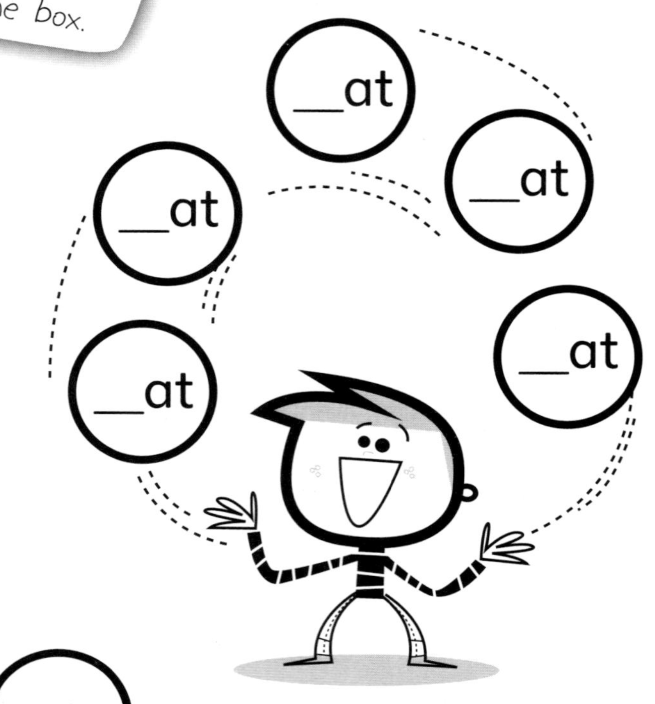

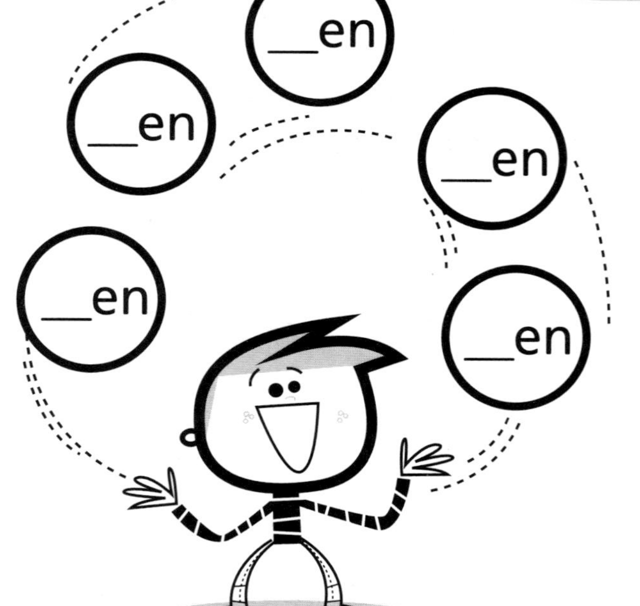

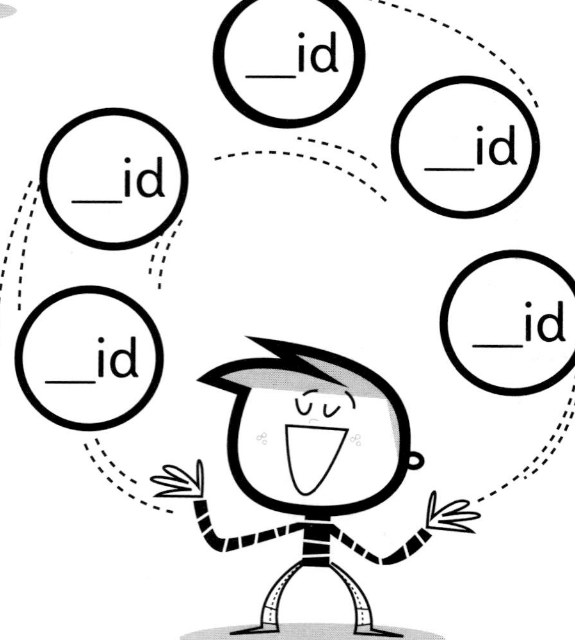

Guided Reading Notes

Creepy Castles

Rapid Level: Stage 2 Set B
NC1B / 5–14A / NI → 2

Lesson Focus:

To tell stories using the voice effectively

Genre: Fiction
Authors: Diana Bentley and Sylvia Karavis
Synopsis: Sir Bold decides to buy an old castle but Hal is worried about the ghosts. Sir Bold does not see any ghosts but Hal can see them everywhere. Finally, Sir Bold sees the ghosts and he and Hal run out of the castle.

Linked photocopiable activity: Page 56
[Writing: Linking split sentences]

Sir Bold and the Haunted Castle

Before Reading

- Share the lesson focus with the group.
- Page 2: Use the *Before Reading* page to introduce the story.

Strategy Check and Reading the Text

- Encourage the children to tackle unfamiliar words by rereading the text to check for sense.
- Ask the children to read independently.
- Select a child to read to you and monitor their progress.

Responding to the Text

Page 13: Use the *Quiz* page to revisit the text. Tell the group to use 'Look Cover Write Check' before spelling the *Super Speller* words.

Assessing the Lesson Focus

- Ask the children to re-tell the story, using appropriate voices for the different characters and situations. Demonstrate by reading page 4, with Sir Bold being very confident.
- Ask the children how they think the characters would speak at the end of the story.

Lesson Focus:

To locate specific information in a text to find answers to simple questions

Genre: Non-fiction
Authors: Diana Bentley and Sylvia Karavis
Synopsis: Many castles were built over 1000 years ago. They were built to protect the owners from their enemies. Some were built on hills, others had tall towers. Some castles are still standing today.

Linked photocopiable activity: Page 57
[Phonics: Spelling CVC words]

Castles

Before Reading

- Share the lesson focus with the group.
- Page14: Use the *Before Reading* page to introduce the text.

Strategy Check and Reading the Text

- Encourage the children to blend consonant clusters at the beginning of unfamiliar words, e.g. page 17 'dr-awbridge'.
- Ask the children to read independently.
- Select a child to read to you and monitor their progress.

Responding to the Text

Page 24: Use the *Quiz* page to revisit the text. Tell the group to use 'Look Cover Write Check' before spelling the *Super Speller* words.

Assessing the Lesson Focus

- Demonstrate how to find information that gives you the answer to a question. Look at page 16. Ask the children why some castles had high towers.
- Ask further questions for the group to find the answers in the text.

Name: ______________________________ Date: ______________

Sir Bold and the Haunted Castle

Join the two parts of the sentences.

Sir Bold read	the castle.
Sir Bold wanted	the notice.
"What about the ghosts?"	into the castle.
Sir Bold and Hal went	said Hal.
They went up	ran away.
They saw a	the tower.
Sir Bold and Hal	ghost.

PCM WRITING

Name: ______________________ Date: ____________

Castles

Make words from the muddled letters.

etg	dre	aht	tno	ist
get	______	______	______	______
ogt	utb	hda	nca	nam
______	______	______	______	______
nme	hmi	gbi	dda	sha
______	______	______	______	______

Today's Dragons

Lesson Focus:

To use talk to organise roles and action

Genre: Non-fiction
Authors: Diana Bentley and Sylvia Karavis
Synopsis: The nearest animal to a story-book dragon is a lizard. Some lizards look a bit like a dragon, some lizards can glide like a dragon and Komodo dragons can even eat people, as dragons do!

Linked photocopiable activity: Page 59
[Phonics: Initial and final letters]

Before Reading

- Share the lesson focus with the group.
- Page 2: Use the *Before Reading* page to introduce the text.

Strategy Check and Reading the Text

- Encourage the children to tackle unfamiliar words by breaking the word into syllables, e.g. page 10 'Kom/o/do'.
- Ask the children to read independently.
- Select a child to read to you and monitor their progress.

Responding to the Text

Page 11: Use the *Quiz* page to revisit the text. Tell the group to use 'Look Cover Write Check' before spelling the *Super Speller* words.

Assessing the Lesson Focus

- Ask the group to discuss how to distribute the text so that everyone has a chance at reading out loud. They could consider two or more children reading at the same time.
- When they have allocated roles, read the text. Evaluate how effective this was.

Sir Bold and the Dragon

Lesson Focus:
To understand the structure of a simple story

Genre: Fiction
Authors: Diana Bentley and Sylvia Karavis
Synopsis: Sir Bold reads about a reward for catching a dragon, so he and Hal set out to do just that! They find it asleep in a cave and Sir Bold says he will capture it, but Hal gets the dragon with his rope. Sir Bold claims the reward but the dragon tells the people it was Hal who got him!

Linked photocopiable activity: Page 60
[Writing: True or False]

Before Reading

- Share the lesson focus with the group.
- Page 12: Use the *Before Reading* page to introduce the story.

Strategy Check and Reading the Text

- Encourage the children to tackle unfamiliar words by rereading the text to check for sense.
- Ask the children to read independently.
- Select a child to read to you and monitor their progress.

Responding to the Text

Page 24: Use the *Quiz* page to revisit the text. Tell the group to use 'Look Cover Write Check' before spelling the *Super Speller* words.

Assessing the Lesson Focus

- Remind the group of the opening of the story.
- Ask them to work with a partner and to tell each other the events in order. What happened in the middle of the story? What happened at the end? Ask the group to re-tell the story from the beginning.

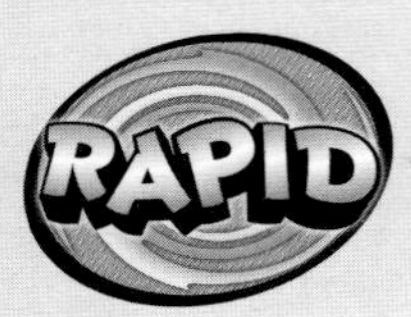

Name: ______________________ Date: ____________

Today's Dragons

Find the matching pairs. Each pair must have the same first and last letters.

The first one has been done for you.

bug bed bad — bed, bad

ran run rim — ______ ______

top ten tin — ______ ______

pit pot hot — ______ ______

man mum men — ______ ______

cot cat got — ______ ______

pan ban pin — ______ ______

Name: ______________________ Date: ____________

Sir Bold and the Dragon

True or False? Circle 'T' or 'F' for the right answer.

	True	False
Sir Bold read the notice.	T	F
The dragon was sleeping in the cave.	T	F
Sir Bold went into the cave first.	T	F
The dragon got Sir Bold.	T	F
Hal got the dragon with his rope.	T	F
The dragon got away.	T	F
The dragon got the reward.	T	F

Knights and Fights

Lesson Focus:

To use intonation when reading

Genre: Fiction
Authors: Diana Bentley and Sylvia Karavis
Synopsis: Sir Bold reads a notice about a tournament – the winner's prize is a bag of gold! He and Sir Crusher begin to fight but Sir Crusher is much stronger. Finally they fight with maces and Sir Crusher falls off his horse and lands upside down on his helmet. Sir Bold is the winner.

Linked photocopiable activity: Page 62 [Writing: Speech bubbles]

Sir Bold and the Tournament

Before Reading

- Share the lesson focus with the group.
- Page 2: Use the *Before Reading* page to introduce the story.

Strategy Check and Reading the Text

- Encourage the children to read ahead in the text to discover what an unfamiliar word might mean.
- Ask the children to read independently.
- Select a child to read to you and monitor their progress.

Responding to the Text

Page 13: Use the *Quiz* page to revisit the text. Tell the group to use 'Look Cover Write Check' before spelling the *Super Speller* words.

Assessing the Lesson Focus

- Talk about reading with intonation and expression. Read pages 4 and 5, first in a monotone, then again with expression.
- Ask individual children to read selected pages to the group. Ask others in the group to evaluate how well the individual read.

Lesson Focus:

To ask and answer questions

Genre: Non-fiction
Authors: Diana Bentley and Sylvia Karavis
Synopsis: Knights had to learn how to fight on horseback. They would ride towards each other with lances, fighting sticks or swords, and try to make the opponent fall off his horse. Sometimes a knight would get killed.

Linked photocopiable activity: Page 63 [Phonics: Adding medial vowels]

Knights and their Weapons

Before Reading

- Share the lesson focus with the group.
- Page 14: Use the *Before Reading* page to introduce the text.

Strategy Check and Reading the Text

- Encourage the children to tackle unfamiliar words by reading ahead in the text to check for sense.
- Ask the children to read independently.
- Select a child to read to you and monitor their progress.

Responding to the Text

Page 24: Use the *Quiz* page to revisit the text. Tell the group to use 'Look Cover Write Check' before spelling the *Super Speller* words.

Assessing the Lesson Focus

- Demonstrate how to ask and answer questions. Show the group page 16: What did knights have to learn to do? Ask them to tell you the words that give the answer.
- Working in pairs, ask the children to work out questions from allocated pages, taking turns to ask and answer the questions.

Name: ______________________ Date: ____________

Sir Bold and the Tournament

Write the speech in the bubbles.

Sir Bold said, “I can win that gold.”

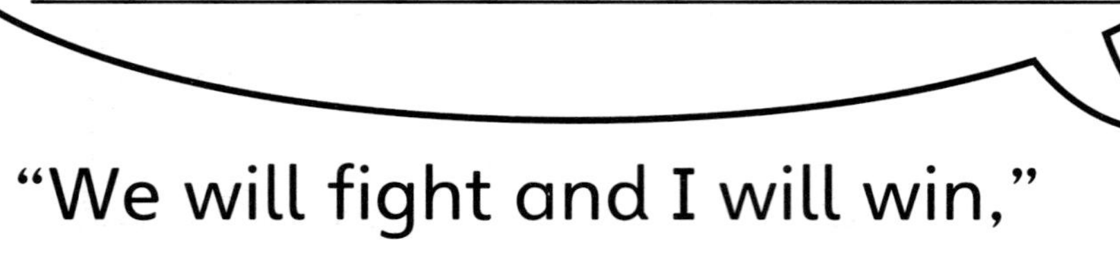

“We will fight and I will win,” said Sir Crusher.

“You have won!” said Hal.

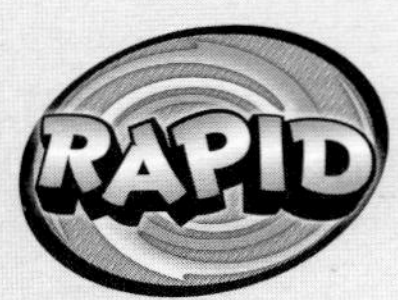

Name: ______________________ Date: ____________

Knights and their Weapons

Add a vowel to make a word.

a e i o u

h__t p__n
t__p d__g
l__t j__g
r__d

b__g t__p
m__n g__t
s__n h__t
j__m

Treasure!

The Search for the Treasure of Tutankhamen

Lesson Focus:
To locate and read significant parts of a recount

Genre: Non-fiction
Authors: Diana Bentley and Sylvia Karavis
Synopsis: Around a hundred years ago, two men went to Egypt to find treasure. They searched for several years, and then they found the greatest treasure in the world – the tomb of Tutankhamen!

Linked photocopiable activity: Page 65
[Phonics: Building CVC words]

Before Reading

- Share the lesson focus with the group.
- Page 2: Use the *Before Reading* page to introduce the text.

Strategy Check and Reading the Text

- Encourage the children to self-correct errors by returning to the start of the sentence and rereading to gain understanding.
- Ask the children to read independently.
- Select a child to read to you and monitor their progress.

Responding to the Text

Page 11: Use the *Quiz* page to revisit the text. Tell the group to use 'Look Cover Write Check' before spelling the *Super Speller* words.

Assessing the Lesson Focus

- Ask the children what they thought was the most exciting part of the account of finding the tomb. Ask them to read the page out loud.
- Look at page 5. What do they think is the most important fact on this page? Repeat with other pages.

Sir Bold and the Gold Cup

Lesson Focus:
To make simple inferences about thoughts and feelings

Genre: Fiction
Authors: Diana Bentley and Sylvia Karavis
Synopsis: Sir Bold reads a notice about a lost gold cup. Whoever finds it can marry the princess. Hal finds the cup but Sir Bold takes it and asks to marry the princess. But the princess refuses; she wants to marry Hal!

Linked photocopiable activity: Page 66
[Writing: Sequencing sentences]

Before Reading

- Share the lesson focus with the group.
- Page 12: Use the *Before Reading* page to introduce the text.

Strategy Check and Reading the Text

- Encourage the children to break unfamiliar words into syllables, e.g. page 13 'prin/cess'.
- Ask the children to read independently.
- Select a child to read to you and monitor their progress.

Responding to the Text

Page 24: Use the *Quiz* page to revisit the text. Tell the group to use 'Look Cover Write Check' before spelling the *Super Speller* words.

Assessing the Lesson Focus

- Ask the children how they think the different characters felt at different points in the story, e.g. page15: How would Sir Bold feel when he could not find the cup? Page 18: How does Hal feel?

Name: ______________________ Date: ____________

The Search for the Treasure of Tutankhamen

Make some words by changing a letter.

The first ones have been done for you.

b	t	f	m	d	p	
n	g	s	c	l	r	h

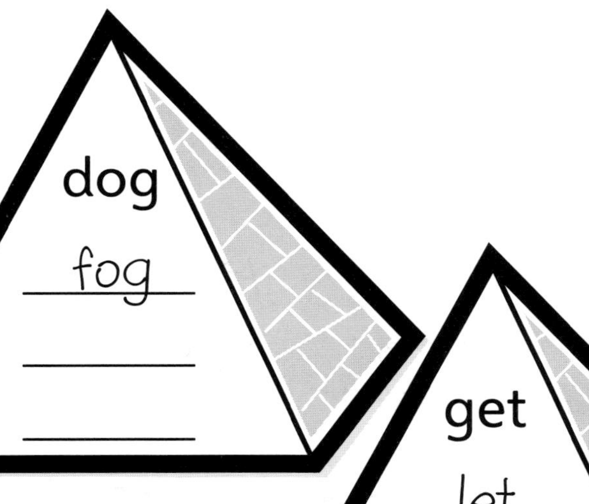

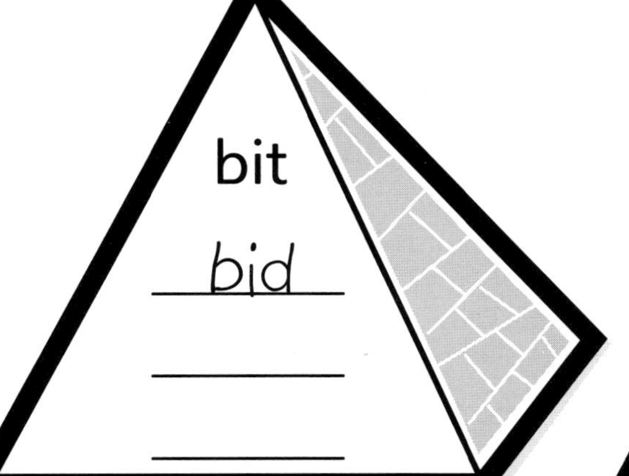

Name: ______________________________ Date: ______________

Sir Bold and the Gold Cup

Put the sentences into the correct order.

Sir Bold said, "I will find the gold cup."

But the gold cup was not in the forest.

Then Hal found the gold cup in the sand.

Sir Bold looked for the gold cup in the forest.

But the princess wanted to marry Hal.

"Now I can marry the princess," said Sir Bold.

But Sir Bold got the cup out of the sand.

Guided Reading Notes

Huge and Hairy

Rapid Level: Stage 3 Set A
NC1A / 5–14 → B / NI 2

Lesson Focus:

To explain or give reasons for their views

Genre: Non-fiction
Authors: Jan Burchett and Sara Vogler
Synopsis: Some people say that there are huge hairy creatures called Bigfoot living in America. Some people say they have seen one. But do they really exist?

Linked photocopiable activity: Page 68 [Phonics: Tracking consonant clusters]

Bigfoot

Before Reading

- Share the lesson focus with the group.
- Page 2: Use the *Before Reading* page to introduce the text.

Strategy Check and Reading the Text

- Encourage the children to self-correct errors by returning to the start of the sentence.
- Ask the children to read independently.
- Select a child to read to you and monitor their progress.

Responding to the Text

Page 11: Use the *Quiz* page to revisit the text. Tell the group to use 'Look Cover Write Check' before spelling the *Super Speller* words.

Assessing the Lesson Focus

Talk to the group about the evidence for the existence of the Bigfoot:

- Ask individual children what they think and why they think this.
- Encourage the children to find evidence from the text.

Lesson Focus:

To take turns to speak and listen to others

Genre: Fiction
Authors: Jan Burchett and Sara Vogler
Synopsis: Jack uses his magic backpack to go to a mountain. He begins to climb it, but soon realises that a Bigfoot is following him. At the top, Jack uses his magic backpack to get away in a hang glider.

Linked photocopiable activity: Page 69 [Writing: Sequencing sentences]

Jack and the Mountain

Before Reading

- Share the lesson focus with the group.
- Page 12: Use the *Before Reading* page to introduce the story.

Strategy Check and Reading the Text

- Encourage the children sound out unfamiliar words by chunking syllables, e.g. page 14 'hel/i/cop/ter'.
- Ask the children to read independently.
- Select a child to read to you and monitor their progress.

Responding to the Text

Page 24: Use the *Quiz* page to revisit the text. Tell the group to use 'Look Cover Write Check' before spelling the *Super Speller* words.

Assessing the Lesson Focus

- Ask the group members to talk about the story: Did they like it? What would they have done in Jack's place?
- Encourage them to listen to each other's views.

Name: ______________________________ Date: ______________

Bigfoot

Can you get away from the Bigfoot?

Circle all the 'br' letter clusters to get to the exit.

dr
dr
br
br
br
br
cr
tr
br
tr
br
br
tr
br
bl
br
br
bl
bl
bl
br
br
pr
tr
br
br
pr
dr
pl
br
pl
br
br
EXIT
br
br
pl

Name: ______________________________ Date: ______________

Jack and the Mountain

Number the sentences in the correct order.

☐	Jack flew in the helicopter to the mountain.
☐	Out of his backback came a helicopter.
☐	The Bigfoot ran up after Jack.
1	Jack wanted to climb a mountain.
☐	Jack got to the top of the mountain.
☐	Jack started to climb the mountain. Then he saw a Bigfoot coming after him.
☐	Out of Jack's backpack came a hang glider.

Beyond the Stars

Lesson Focus:
To make simple inferences about thoughts and feelings and reasons for actions

Genre: Fiction
Authors: Jan Burchett and Sara Vogler
Synopsis: Jack's magic backpack takes him to Planet Spot. He looks for aliens but when he finds them, they seem very hungry! Jack gets back into his spaceship – fast!

Linked photocopiable activity: Page 71
[Writing: High-frequency words]

Jack on Planet Spot

Before Reading

- Share the lesson focus with the group.
- Page 2: Use the *Before Reading* page to introduce the story.

Strategy Check and Reading the Text

- Encourage the children to tackle unfamiliar words by rereading the text to check for sense.
- Ask the children to read independently.
- Select a child to read to you and monitor their progress.

Responding to the Text

Page 13: Use the *Quiz* page to revisit the text. Tell the group to use 'Look Cover Write Check' before spelling the *Super Speller* words.

Assessing the Lesson Focus

Ask individual children to decide how Jack feels:

- Page 3: At the start of the story.
- Page 12: When he gets home.

Lesson Focus:
 To explain or give reasons for their views

Genre: Non-fiction
Authors: Jan Burchett and Sara Vogler
Synopsis: The nine planets in our solar system are not like Earth. Mercury is boiling hot during the day, Mars is freezing cold, and some of the planets have strong winds, lumps of ice, and smell bad!

Linked photocopiable activity: Page 72
[Phonics: Initial consonant clusters]

The Planets

Before Reading

- Share the lesson focus with the group.
- Page 14: Use the *Before Reading* page to introduce the text.

Strategy Check and Reading the Text

- Encourage the children to break up unfamiliar words into syllables and sound them out, e.g. page 20 'Sa/turn', and page 21 'Nep/tune'.
- Ask the children to read independently.
- Select a child to read to you and monitor their progress.

Responding to the Text

Page 24: Use the *Quiz* page to revisit the text. Tell the group to use 'Look Cover Write Check' before spelling the *Super Speller* words.

Assessing the Lesson Focus

- Ask the group to look through the text again and decide which planet they would like to visit, or which one they would not like to visit, giving reasons for their answers.

Name: ____________________________ Date: ____________

Jack on Planet Spot

Circle the word 'were'. Can you find 10?

were	when	were	where	was	when
were	why	were	which	when	were
went	here	where	were	was	here
were	where	which	were	why	which
when	were	went	west	were	here

Circle the word 'out'. Can you find 10?

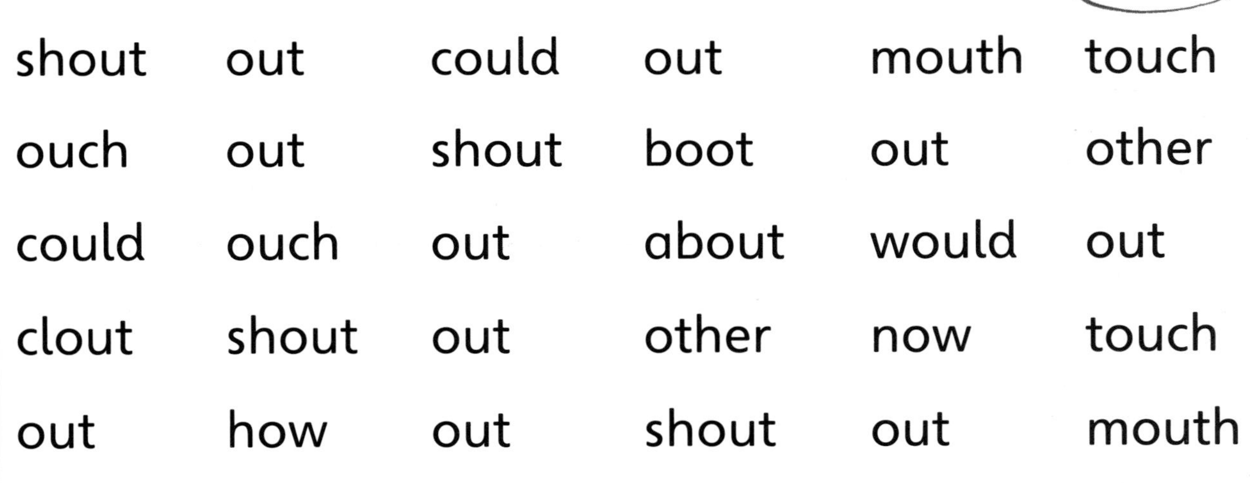

shout	out	could	out	mouth	touch
ouch	out	shout	boot	out	other
could	ouch	out	about	would	out
clout	shout	out	other	now	touch
out	how	out	shout	out	mouth

Choose 'were' or 'Out' to complete each sentence.

Jack saw there ______ aliens on Planet Spot.

______ of his backpack came a spaceship.

Name: ______________________ Date: __________

The Planets

Add these consonant clusters to make words.

bl br cr dr
fl pl sl sm
st sw tr

Savage Beasts

Lesson Focus:

 To respond to and evaluate a text

Genre: Fiction
Authors: Jan Burchett and Sara Vogler
Synopsis: Jack uses his magic backpack to visit Africa. He looks for hippos, lions and snakes but he cannot see any. In his tent, he sees a terrible shadow, so he packs up and runs away. But it was only a tiny spider!

Linked photocopiable activity: Page 74
[Writing: Word order in sentences]

Jack in Africa

Before Reading

- Share the lesson focus with the group.
- Page 2: Use the *Before Reading* page to introduce the story.

Strategy Check and Reading the Text

- Encourage the children to self-correct errors by returning to the start of a sentence.
- Ask the children to read independently.
- Select a child to read to you and monitor their progress.

Responding to the Text

Page 13: Use the *Quiz* page to revisit the text. Tell the group to use 'Look Cover Write Check' before spelling the *Super Speller* words.

Assessing the Lesson Focus

- Discuss what is really happening in this story.
- What do the group think is the funniest episode?
- Have they read any other story similar to this one?
- What fierce animals would they like to see?
- Did they enjoy this story? What did they like /dislike about it?

Lesson Focus:

 To locate and read significant parts of a recount

Genre: Non-fiction
Authors: Jan Burchett and Sara Vogler
Synopsis: There are some very fierce animals in the world. Which one is the most dangerous – the snake, the hippo, the crocodile, the lion, or the spider? No; it is the mosquito.

Linked photocopiable activity: Page 75
[Phonics: Initial consonant clusters]

Fierce Animals

Before Reading

- Share the lesson focus with the group.
- Page 14: Use the *Before Reading* page to introduce the text.

Strategy Check and Reading the Text

- Encourage the children to tackle unfamiliar words by blending the intial consonant cluster, e.g. page 15 'sn-ake' and page 18 'cr-ocodile'.
- Ask the children to read independently.
- Select a child to read to you and monitor their progress.

Responding to the Text

Page 24: Use the *Quiz* page to revisit the text. Tell the group to use 'Look Cover Write Check' before spelling the *Super Speller* words.

Assessing the Lesson Focus

- Talk about the facts on page 15. What makes a snake dangerous?
- Ask individual children to read allocated pages and tell the group what makes the animals dangerous to humans.

Name: ______________________ Date: ____________

Jack in Africa

Sort out the muddled sentences.

Jack said, “want I some fierce to animals see.”

Jack said, “______________________________.”

Jack said, “get I’ll my and backpack go Africa to.”

Jack said, “______________________________.”

Jack hippos wanted see some to.

Jack ______________________________.

POP! of backpack Out map a came his.

POP! ______________________________.

Jack said, “no hippos There here are.”

Jack said, “______________________________.”

Name: ______________________ Date: __________

Fierce Animals

Circle the correct cluster to match the picture.

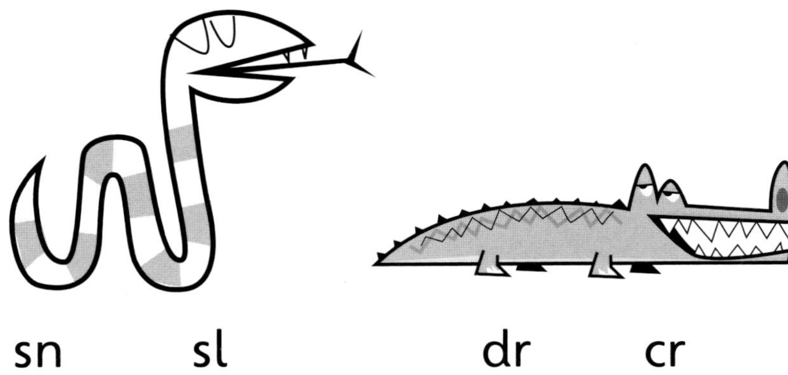

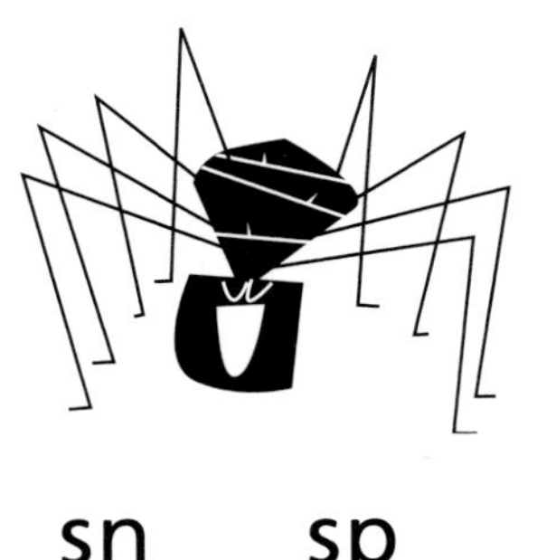

sn sl

dr cr

sn sp

fr thr

fl tr

dr br

Add the correct cluster: cr, sn, sp.

A ____ake bite can kill you. 

A ____ocodile can kill you. 

A ____ider can kill you. 

Under the Sea

Funny, Weird and Scary

Lesson Focus:

 To ask and answer questions

Genre: Non-fiction
Authors: Jan Burchett and Sara Vogler
Synopsis: The deep sea contains many funny, weird and scary animals, including the leafy sea dragon, the giant deep sea spider, the pufferfish and the hammerhead shark.

Linked photocopiable activity: Page 77
[Phonics: Initial consonant clusters]

Before Reading

- Share the lesson focus with the group.
- Page 2: Use the *Before Reading* page to introduce the text.

Strategy Check and Reading the Text

- Encourage the children to sound out unfamiliar words by breaking them into syllables, e.g. page 9 'ham/mer/head'.
- Ask the children to read independently.
- Select a child to read to you and monitor their progress.

Responding to the Text

Page 11: Use the *Quiz* page to revisit the text. Tell the group to use 'Look Cover Write Check' before spelling the *Super Speller* words.

Assessing the Lesson Focus

- Demonstrate to the group how to ask and answer questions. Look at page 3. Ask the children to identify the question. Ask them what the leafy sea dragon does if a big fish wants to eat it.
- Ask the children to devise questions and challenge the others in the group to find the answers.

Jack and the Wreck

Lesson Focus:

 To use intonation when reading

Genre: Fiction
Authors: Jan Burchett and Sara Vogler
Synopsis: Jack uses his magic backpack to take him to the bottom of the sea in a submarine. He finds a treasure chest there, but needs a key. Something gives him a key. Then Jack realises that it is a shark, and gets away – fast!

Linked photocopiable activity: Page 78
[Writing: High-frequency words]

Before Reading

- Share the lesson focus with the group.
- Page 12: Use the *Before Reading* page to introduce the story.

Strategy Check and Reading the Text

- Encourage the children to tackle unfamiliar words by rereading the text to check for sense.
- Ask the children to read independently.
- Select a child to read to you and monitor their progress.

Responding to the Text

Page 24: Use the *Quiz* page to revisit the text. Tell the group to use 'Look Cover Write Check' before spelling the *Super Speller* words.

Assessing the Lesson Focus

- Read pages 13-15 in a monotone. Ask the group to tell you where to put emphasis, and whether to change your voice when Jack is speaking.
- Ask individual children to read pages 16-17 and 22-23. Can they make these pages sound different, for effect?

Name: ______________________________ Date: ____________

Funny, Weird and Scary

Fill in the gaps in the sentences using the words in the box.

dragon	bright	spider	scary	swim	small	plate

The leafy sea ________ lives deep down in the sea.

It does not ________ very fast.

The deep sea ________ is very big.

It is as big as a ________ .

The angler fish has a ________ light on its head.

It eats ________ fish.

Do you think it is funny, weird or ________ ?

Name: ______________________ Date: ____________

Jack and the Wreck

Fill in the gaps in the sentences using the words in the box.

into	Out	gave	saw	said	could	looked	want

"I _______ to explore a wreck," said Jack.

POP! _______ of his backpack came a submarine.

Then Jack _______ a wreck.

He went _______ the wreck.

He saw a treasure chest but he _______ not open it.

Something _______ Jack a key.

Jack _______ over his shoulder and saw a shark.

"Aaargh!" _______ Jack and he zoomed away.

Guided Reading Notes
Big Bangs!

Lesson Focus:

 To tell stories using the voice effectively

Genre: Fiction
Author: Haydn Middleton
Synopsis: Jim sees fireworks and convinces Captain Crab that the people have left their houses open while they watch the fireworks. The pirates go to steal their gold – then they realise that the 'fireworks' are really a volcano erupting!

Linked photocopiable activity: Page 80
[Writing: Word order in sentences]

Jim and the Fireworks

Before Reading

- Share the lesson focus with the group.
- Page 2: Use the *Before Reading* page to introduce the story.

Strategy Check and Reading the Text

- Encourage the children to read ahead in the text to discover what the meaning of an unfamiliar word might be.
- Ask the children to read independently.
- Select a child to read to you and monitor their progress.

Responding to the Text

Page 13: Use the *Quiz* page to revisit the text. Tell the group to use 'Look Cover Write Check' before spelling the *Super Speller* words.

Assessing the Lesson Focus

- Working in pairs, the children re-tell the story to each other, thinking how to sound persuasive, excited, frightened, etc.
- Ask pairs of children to re-tell the story. The group should evaluate how well they used their voices.

Lesson Focus:
To locate and read significant parts of a recount

Genre: Non-fiction
Author: Haydn Middleton
Synopsis: When a volcano erupts it makes a very big bang and it looks like fireworks in the sky. But volcanoes are very dangerous. They can destroy homes and land. Two famous volcanoes are Mount Pinatubo and Krakatoa.

Linked photocopiable activity: Page 81
[Phonics: Final consonant clusters]

Volcanoes

Before Reading

- Share the lesson focus with the group.
- Page14: Use the *Before Reading* page to introduce the text.

Strategy Check and Reading the Text

- Encourage the children to sound out unfamiliar words by breaking them into syllables, e.g. page 15 'vol/ca/no', and page 20 'Pin/a/tu/bo'.
- Ask the children to read independently.
- Select a child to read to you and monitor their progress.

Responding to the Text

Page 24: Use the *Quiz* page to revisit the text.Tell the group to use 'Look Cover Write Check' before spelling the *Super Speller* words.

Assessing the Lesson Focus

- Page 15: Demonstrate how to select important information from the text (e.g. A volcano is a mountain that erupts).
- Ask individual children to tell you what they think is important information from other selected pages.

Name: ______________________ Date: ______________

Jim and the Fireworks

Sort out the muddled sentences.

Pirate Jim a sky saw flash the in.

Pirate Jim ______________________________________.

All the pirates the went see to fireworks.

All the pirates ______________________________________.

The people left have island the.

The people ______________________________________.

We could their go grab and gold.

We could ______________________________________.

The people shouting in were boats the.

The people ______________________________________.

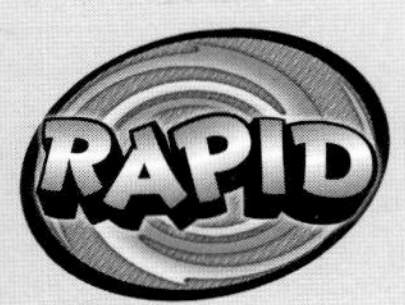

Name: ______________________ Date: ____________

Volcanoes

Add the word beginnings to the consonant clusters.

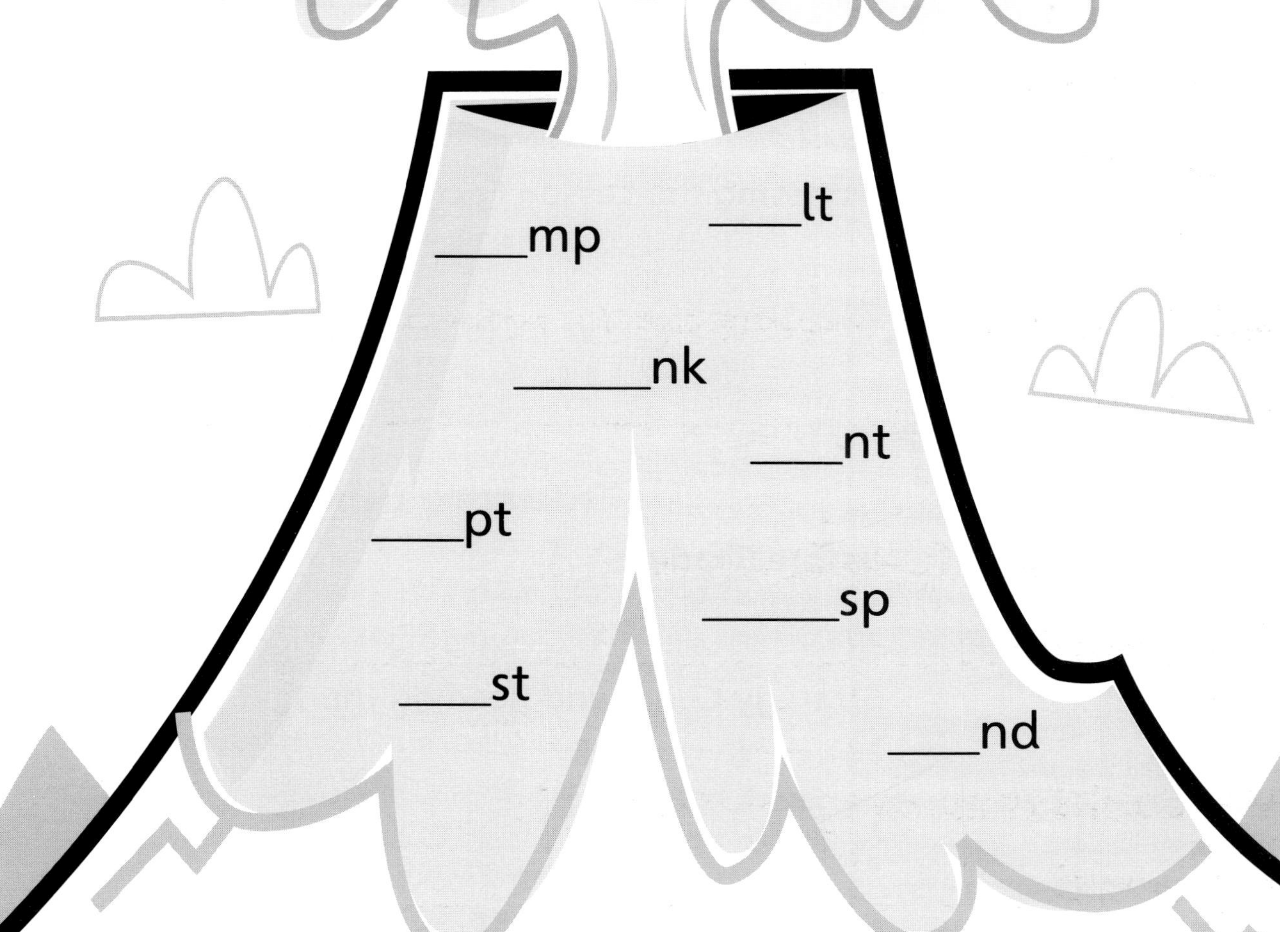

Now write each word again.

__________ __________ __________ __________

__________ __________ __________ __________

Guided Reading Notes

What a Monster!

Rapid Level: Stage 3 Set B
NC1A / 5–14 → B / NI 2

Make-Believe Monsters

Lesson Focus:
To break up words into syllables

Genre: Non-fiction
Author: Haydn Middleton
Synopsis: People have made up stories about monsters for thousands of years. Famous monsters include the Centaur, the Cyclops, the Hydra and Medusa. All of these monsters do not like humans, and the Minotaur even likes to eat children!

Linked photocopiable activity: Page 83
[Phonics: Final consonant clusters]

Before Reading

- Share the lesson focus with the group.
- Page 2: Use the *Before Reading* page to introduce the text.

Strategy Check and Reading the Text

- Encourage the children to look for known parts of an unfamiliar word, and using these to produce the whole word.
- Ask the children to read independently.
- Select a child to read to you and monitor their progress.

Responding to the Text

Page 11: Use the *Quiz* page to revisit the text. Tell the group to use 'Look Cover Write Check' before spelling the *Super Speller* words.

Assessing the Lesson Focus

- Look at the names of the monsters and the pronunciation guide. Page 3: How many syllables can the children hear in the name?
- Select other polysyllabic words for the group to count the syllables. Explain how breaking words into syllables can help with spelling.
- Invite individual children to read some of the monsters' names.

Treasure Island

Lesson Focus:
To predict events and outcomes in a story

Genre: Fiction
Author: Haydn Middleton
Synopsis: Pirate Jim sees a baby dragon with a box of treasure on an island. Captain Crab and the pirates decide to steal the treasure. They sleep overnight on the island but they are cold. To get warm they burn the treasure box but then they discover they are on the back of the baby dragon's dad!

Linked photocopiable activity: Page 84
[Writing: Making CVCC words]

Before Reading

- Share the lesson focus with the group.
- Page 12: Use the *Before Reading* page to introduce the story.

Strategy Check and Reading the Text

- Encourage the children to self-correct errors by returning to the start of the sentence.
- Ask the children to read independently.
- Select a child to read to you and monitor their progress.

Responding to the Text

Page 24: Use the *Quiz* page to revisit the text. Tell the group to use 'Look Cover Write Check' before spelling the *Super Speller* words.

Assessing the Lesson Focus

- Ask the group if they worked out what was going to happen at the end.
- What were the clues in the text on pages 16 and 17? What clues were there in the illustrations?

Name: ______________________ Date: ____________

Make-Believe Monsters

Make some words ending with a consonant cluster.

-nd
-lt
-sk
-nt

-mp
-sk
-st
-ft

bend ______ ______ ______ ______ ______

-pt
-st
-nk
-ft

-ft
-sp
-nt
-dge

______ ______ ______ ______ ______ ______

Name: ______________________ Date: ______________

Treasure Island

Use the word beginnings and consonant clusters to make some words.

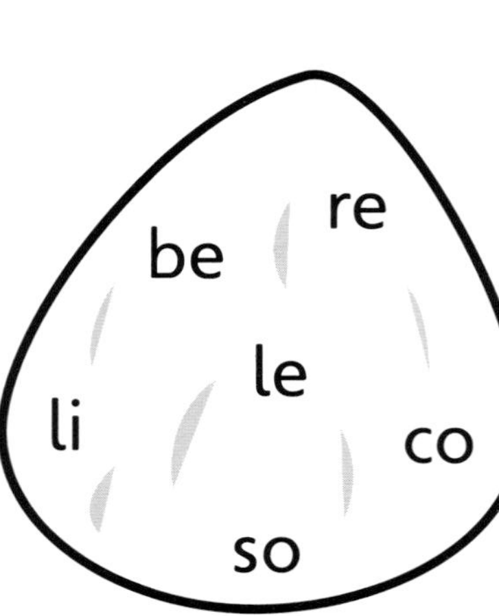

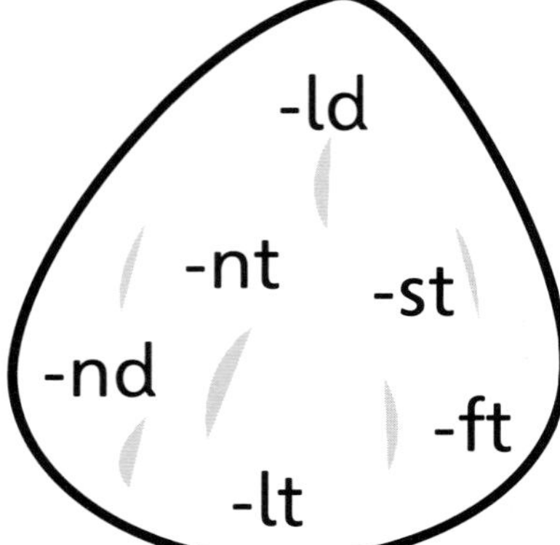

Now write one new word for each consonant cluster.

__nd __ld __nt __lt __ft __st

Jelly Trouble

Rapid Level: Stage 3 Set B
NC1A / 5–14 → B / NI 2

Lesson Focus:

To use intonation and expression when reading

Genre: Fiction
Author: Haydn Middleton
Synopsis: Jim persuades Captain Crab to attack another ship, but it has no treasure. Then they fire at their own ship to stop it from sailing away. But it starts to sink so they have to throw their own treasure overboard to save it.

Linked photocopiable activity: Page 86 [Writing: Reading for meaning]

Give Us Our Ship Back!

Before Reading

- Share the lesson focus with the group.
- Page 2: Use the *Before Reading* page to introduce the story.

Strategy Check and Reading the Text

- Encourage the children to tackle unfamiliar words by rereading the text to check for sense.
- Ask the children to read independently.
- Select a child to read to you and monitor their progress.

Responding to the Text

Page13: Use the *Quiz* page to revisit the text. Tell the group to use 'Look Cover Write Check' before spelling the *Super Speller* words.

Assessing the Lesson Focus

- Ask individual children to read as Jim, Captain Crab, Polly, narrator. Encourage them to read with expression and intonation.
- Invite the rest of the group to evaluate their reading.

Lesson Focus:
To take notice of punctuation when reading

Genre: Non-fiction
Author: Haydn Middleton
Synopsis: Jellyfish are made mostly of water. Some jellyfish are colourful, whereas some have no colour. Some jellyfish even sting people.

Linked photocopiable activity: Page 87 [Phonics: Making CVCC words]

Jellyfish

Before Reading

- Share the lesson focus with the group.
- Page 14: Use the *Before Reading* page to introduce the text.

Strategy Check and Reading the Text

- Encourage the children to sound out unfamiliar words by chunking syllables, e.g. page 20 'je/lly/fish' and 'ten/ta/cles'.
- Ask the children to read independently.
- Select a child to read to you and monitor their progress.

Responding to the Text

Page 24: Use the *Quiz* page to revisit the text. Tell the group to use 'Look Cover Write Check' before spelling the *Super Speller* words.

Assessing the Lesson Focus

- Read page 15 to the group. Discuss the punctuation and explain how this helped you to read the text.
- Ask individual children to read different pages, observing punctuation. Ask other children to see if the readers are taking notice of punctuation.

Name: ______________________________ Date: ______________

Give Us Our Ship Back!

Read Jim's ideas and decide if they are Good or Bad.

I want more treasure.	Good	Bad
Let's get the treasure from the *Jellyfish*.	Good	Bad
I'll fire a cannonball to stop the *Jellyfish* pirates.	Good	Bad
Throw out something heavy.	Good	Bad
Throw out the treasure.	Good	Bad
Does Pirate Jim have good ideas?	Yes	No

Name: ______________________ Date: ______________

Jellyfish

Join the word beginnings to the endings.

Then write the words below.

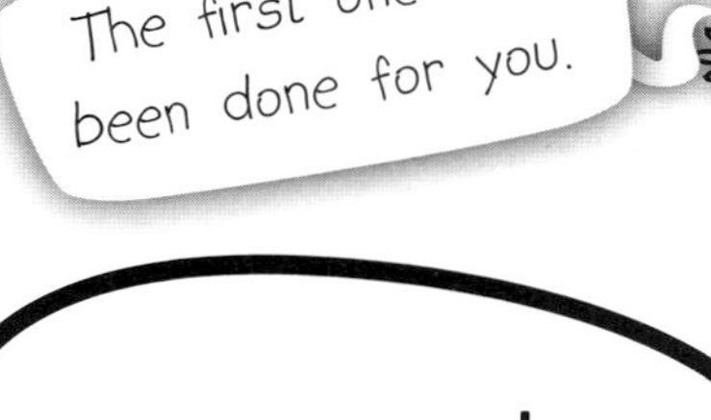

ju bu
-mp
tu du

so ta
-ft
gi le

lo se
-nt
be we

co so
-ld
go ra

-mp	-ft	-nt	-ld
jump	________	________	________
________	________	________	________
________	________	________	________

PCM PHONICS

Guided Reading Notes
Ship Shape

Rapid Level: Stage 3 Set B
NC1A / 5–14 → B / NI 2

Life at Sea

Lesson Focus:

 To ask and answer questions

Genre: Non-fiction
Author: Haydn Middleton
Synopsis: Long ago, life on board a sailing ship was very hard. The sailors were often away from home for years. The food went bad, many sailors fell overboard and drowned, and sometimes pirates would attack the ships.

Linked photocopiable activity: Page 89 [Phonics: Making CVCC words]

Before Reading

- Share the lesson focus with the group.
- Page 2: Use the *Before Reading* page to introduce the text.

Strategy Check and Reading the Text

- Encourage the children to tackle unfamiliar words by rereading the text to check for sense.
- Ask the children to read independently.
- Select a child to read to you and monitor their progress.

Responding to the Text

Page 11: Use the *Quiz* page to revisit the text. Tell the group to use 'Look Cover Write Check' before spelling the *Super Speller* words.

Assessing the Lesson Focus

- Page 3: Read the page and then demonstrate to the group how to ask questions. For example, "What was life at sea like?"
- Allocate different pages to different pairs. Ask them to work out a question for the rest of the group to answer.

The Treasure Map

Lesson Focus:
To predict events from the text

Genre: Fiction
Author: Haydn Middleton
Synopsis: Jim sees an island and persuades Captain Crab to look for hidden treasure on it. Jim finds a map with a cross on it and tells the pirates to dig! But Polly sees that it is not a map, but a torn piece of paper from a noughts and crosses game!

Linked photocopiable activity: Page 90 [Writing: Reading for meaning]

Before Reading

- Share the lesson focus with the group.
- Page12: Use the *Before Reading* page to introduce the story.

Strategy Check and Reading the Text

- Encourage the children to self-correct errors by returning to the start of the sentence and rereading to gain understanding.
- Ask the children to read independently.
- Select a child to read to you and monitor their progress.

Responding to the Text

Page 24: Use the *Quiz* page to revisit the text. Tell the group to use 'Look Cover Write Check' before spelling the *Super Speller* words.

Assessing the Lesson Focus

- Discuss with the group if they predicted what was going to happen.
- Page 18: Would they have believed the 'map' was a treasure map?
- Page 21: Did they guess what the 'map' really was?

Name: ______________________ Date: ____________

Life at Sea

Choose consonant clusters to end the words.

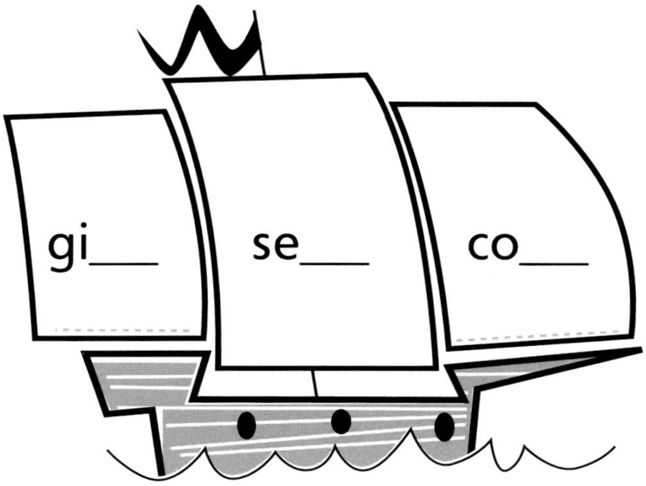

gi___ se___ co___

nk ft nd st

we___ bu___ so___

nd mp ft nt

lo___ ha___ bli___

nd sk nk st

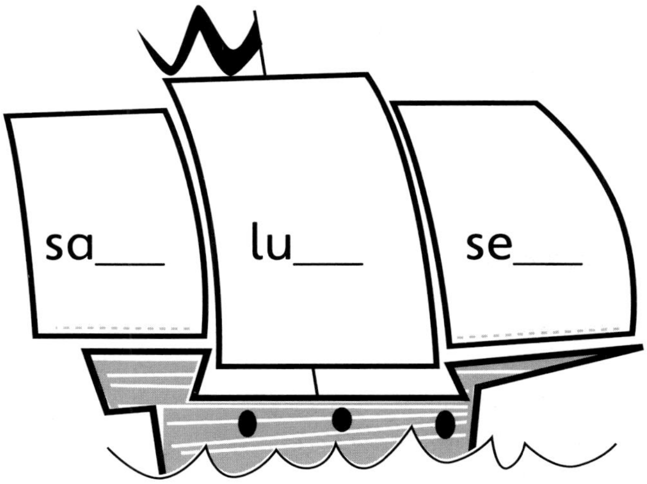

sa___ lu___ se___

mp nt lt nk

Now write the words in these lists.

-nt	-st	-nd	-mp	-nk	-ft
_____	_____	_____	_____	_____	_____
_____	_____	_____	_____	_____	_____

Name: ______________________ Date: ____________

The Treasure Map

Underline the extra word in each sentence.
Then write the extra words to make a secret message.

(1) Let's go to the the island.

(2) Pirates hide their treasure treasure on islands.

(3) The pirates looked but is they found no treasure.

(4) Jim found a bit of under paper.

(5) It a is the treasure map.

(6) It is just a torn tree bit of paper.

Secret message

(1) ______ (2) ______ (3) ______ (4) ______ (5) ______ (6) ______

Assessment for Learning

In order for children to become confident and competent readers, it is important that they are engaged in the process of learning. Too often, struggling readers have little idea of the purpose of the tasks they undertake and have not had the opportunity to reflect upon reasons why they may find reading difficult.

Struggling readers make the best progress when support is:

- systematic
- regular
- paced

and when learning intentions are shared.

How does *Rapid* meet Assessment for Learning goals?

Pupils are encouraged to share in their learning in a number of ways:

The *Rapid* texts

- The *Before Reading* page ensures the pupil is focused on the task ahead.
- The *Quiz* page ensures the pupil reflects upon their reading.

The Guided Reading notes and Photocopy Master (PCM) worksheets

- The Guided Reading notes and PCMs identify a learning intention.

The Child Self-Assessment Chart

- The 'My Reading Progress Chart' on page 110 gives the pupil the opportunity to reflect upon their learning, celebrate success, and to identify where they still need help. This process of self-evaluation helps to engage the learner with their own achievement. It is based on a very positive model of 'I can ...' since so many struggling readers lack self-confidence and have little vision of themselves as readers.

The Key Word Assessment Bookmarks

- The key word assessment bookmarks on page 111 provide a quick checklist of the key words introduced at each *Rapid* Stage. The words are selected from the relevant Set of each Stage and are chosen for their value as high-frequency words.

The *Rapid Reading Assistant* software

- The 'Read and Record' feature offers the opportunity for pupils to self-monitor their progress, as an aid to independent learning. A pupil can do this by independently reading a text on-screen, recording their reading as they go. The software tracks this reading performance and a 'review' feature highlights words using a colour code system. This shows the pupil (and teacher) which words were read well and which words need further work.
- The *Rapid Reading Assistant* software also encourages pupils to collect 'Power Points' for their reading performances and quiz answers. The scores are collated on a certificate and this reward system is an ideal way for pupils to share in their own learning.

Benchmark Assessment

In addition to all the formative assessment provided by *Rapid*, there is also the opportunity for summative assessment in the form of 'Running Records' and 'Comprehension, Phonic and Spelling Records'. The summative assessment is presented in the form of benchmark books – called *Rapid* Assessment Books.

Aims of the Assessment Books

All schools have to provide data related to Special Educational Needs readers. This data should be accurate, easy to acquire and informative.

Running records are generally agreed to be extremely effective in providing evidence of pupil progress. One of the advantages of running records is that they fit comfortably alongside teaching methods, so the testing evolves quite naturally from the reading. It is also a form of assessment that is familiar to many pupils, and it is non-threatening as it parallels any normal reading session. The data from the running records can be used to:

- determine whether a pupil is ready for the next Stage of *Rapid*
- provide feedback to the pupil
- provide evidence of pupil progress for tracking purposes.

The *Rapid* Assessment Books

There are six *Rapid* Assessment Books, covering the whole programme. Each book contains two assessment texts (one for Set A and one for Set B). The 'Running Records' and 'Comprehension, Phonics and Spelling Records' for the three Assessment Books for Stages 1-3 of *Rapid* are covered within this Teaching Guide.

- All the assessment texts are fiction and are based on the relevant characters that the pupils will have met in the Reading Books of the programme.
- The format of the assessment is identical to the core Reading Books, including a *Before Reading* page and a *Quiz* page.
- Each assessment text has been carefully chosen to practise the vocabulary introduced in the core Reading Books. Only a very limited number of 'new' words is included in the stories (only six per text in Stages 1-3). In addition, a very small number of phonically-decodable CVC words (e.g. did, fed) is also included.

The *Quiz* pages for the assessment texts differ slightly from those in the Reading Books. This is in order to assess comprehension, and phonic and spelling skills as fully as possible, as follows:

- There are three different forms of comprehension questions: literal, inferential, and those that draw a personal response.
- Word-level assessment covers only the phonic focus relevant to a particular Set.
- *Super Speller* words are to be spelled from memory.

Assessing Reading with *Rapid*

The following section provides comprehensive guidance on *Rapid's* benchmark assessment, giving step-by-step instructions on how to assess a pupil's reading progress.

Rapid benchmark assessment covers reading accuracy as well as comprehension, phonics and spelling:

1. **Running Records** (See *Rapid* Running Record PCMs)
   Running records provide an accurate picture of how well a pupil can read a text. They reveal which independent reading skills a pupil has mastered and which reading strategies he or she is using. Listening to a pupil read and marking any errors that occur enables the adult systematically to assess where a pupil needs help.
2. **Checking Comprehension, Phonics and Spelling**
   (See *Rapid* Comprehension, Phonics and Spelling Record PCMs)
   It is also essential to ensure that a pupil has read with understanding. Discussing the text after reading enables the adult to assess whether a pupil has read with understanding.

How to do a benchmark assessment

Setting up the assessment reading session

You will need:

- The assessment book for the appropriate level
- The 'Running Record' and 'Comprehension, Phonics and Spelling Record' PCMs (see pages 98–109)
- Pencil / pen.

Before Reading:

- The pupil sits beside the adult.
- Record the pupil's name, and date of the assessment.
- Give the pupil the book and explain that you want him/her to read aloud.
- Explain that you are going to see how well he/she can manage without prompts from you.

During Reading:

- Introduce the book by looking at the cover and the title page.
- Remind the pupil that he/she has met the characters in previous texts.
- Look at the *Before Reading* page for the appropriate text.
- Go over the Tricky words and explain that you will help with these words.
- Read the Story starter.
- Ask the pupil to start reading.

How to do a benchmark assessment

Marking the Running Record PCM

- Tick each correctly-read word.

Do <u>not</u> count the following as errors:

- If the pupil self-corrects an error, write 'Sc' above the text (NB This is not counted as an error).
- If the pupil repeats a word, write 'R' over the word (NB This is not counted as an error).

Count the following miscues as errors:

- If the pupil <u>omits</u> a word, write 'O' above the word.
- If the pupil <u>inserts</u> a word, write in the word.
- If you have to <u>tell</u> the child a word, write 'T' over the word.
- If the pupil attempts the word, write the attempt over the word and record it as an error unless the pupil manages to say the word correctly.
- If the pupil appears confused, ask the pupil to start again from the beginning of the sentence, and record this as one error unless the words are incorrect a second time.

Reading strategies

Use the following codes to record the strategies the pupil uses to tackle a word:

Ph = phonic	the pupil tries to sound out the problem word
G = graphic	the pupil suggests a word that looks similar to the problem word
S = syntactic	the pupil suggests a grammatically sensible word
C = contextual	the pupil suggests a sensible substitution within the meaning of the text as a whole
SC= self-corrects	the pupil realises that he/she has strayed from the text and goes back and rereads correctly. If he/she goes back but continues to read incorrectly, mark the words as errors.

Words assessed

- You may like to note the actual miscues in the 'Words assessed' column by marking a dot next to the relevant word/s.

Marking the Comprehension, Phonics and Spelling Record PCM

After Reading

- Use the *Quiz* page 'Text Detective' to check for comprehension. Give 3 marks for a full answer. Give 0 to any answer that shows lack of understanding. Allocate 1 or 2 marks for answers that fall between this range.
- Use the *Quiz* page 'Word Detective' to assess phonic knowledge. Give 1 mark for each correct response. Give 0 for any wrong answer.
- Use the *Quiz* page 'Super Speller' to check on spelling of high-frequency words. Give 1 mark for each word correctly spelled. Give 0 for any error in the spelling.
- Share the joke with the pupil!

Identifying a pupil's reading level

Running Record Results

To gather the results of the running record, use the following steps:

1. Count the number of miscues (errors) in the reading and record these in the 'Total miscues' box on the Running Record PCM.
2. Use this total miscue result to determine the percentage accuracy rate using the tables below. (There is one table for *Rapid* Stages 1 and 2, and one for *Rapid* Stage 3.) Simply find the number of miscues in the top row of the correct table, and find the accuracy rate in the bottom row.

Determining Accuracy Rate

More than **5** miscues at Stages 1 and 2, and more than **10** at Stage 3, indicates that the pupil is not ready to progress to the next Set in the *Rapid* programme.

Stages 1 and 2 (50 Running Words)

Miscue total	1	2	3	4	5	6	7	8	9	10
Accuracy rate	98%	96%	94%	92%	90%	88%	86%	84%	82%	80%

Stage 3 (100 Running Words)

Miscue total	1	2	3	4	5	6	7	8	9	10	11	12	13	14	15
Accuracy rate	99%	98%	97%	96%	95%	94%	93%	92%	91%	90%	89%	88%	87%	86%	85%

Comprehension, Phonics and Spelling Record Results

To interpret these results, use the following chart:

Area of understanding	Score	Action
Comprehension	7–9	Acceptable for Set
	Below 7	Pupil will require greater reading practice at this level. The pupil should not move up to next *Rapid* level.
Phonics	3	Acceptable for Set
	Below 3	• Target phonic knowledge in individual or group work • Use the phonic-based PCMs for further practice The pupil should still move up to next *Rapid* level.
Spelling	2–3	Acceptable for Set
	Below 2	• Target spelling knowledge in individual and group work • Use the spelling-based PCMs for further practice The pupil should still move up to next *Rapid* level.

How do I use the assessment results?

Use the results from both the Running Record and from the Comprehension, Phonics and Spelling Record to assess whether a pupil is ready to move to the next level of *Rapid*, using the following guidelines:

- Pupils reading at a 90+% accuracy rate and scoring 7+ for Comprehension, Phonics and Spelling are ready to progress to the next *Rapid* level.
- Pupils scoring below these rates will need further practice at the same *Rapid* level.

Example of a completed *Rapid* Running Record

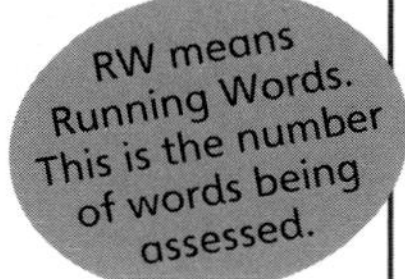

Name: Michael Date: 12 October

Story: **Rugby Run** RW = 50

Page	*Shaded words are not assessed*	Strategies used	Words assessed • = miscues
7	"I can stop him," said Tom. "No, Tom," said Kim. "The man is too big. You can't stop him."	Ph G	I can stop • him said • no the man is too big you can't •
8	Tom ran at the robber. The robber ran fast, but Tom ran faster.	Ph	ran at but
9	Tom got the robber. "Got you!" he said. "Aaargh!" said the robber.		got he
10	A policeman saw Tom. "Good job, Tom," said the policeman. "I saw you stop the robber."	G G	a saw • good • job
11	"Good job, Tom," said Kim. "You got the robber. You can run fast."		
12	"Yes," said Tom. "I can run fast." "I *am* good at rugby!"		

Key:

T = told O = omitted Sc = self-corrects

Strategies: Ph = phonic G = graphic S = syntactic C = contextual

Total miscues: 5

RAPID

Example of a completed *Rapid* Comprehension, Phonics and Spelling Record

Name: Michael Date: 12 October

Story: **Rugby Run**

Text Detective

Questions to check understanding **Response (1 – 3)**

Literal recall

What did the robber steal from the lady?

He stole her handbag. 3

Inferential comprehension

Why did Tom say he was good at rugby?

Because he could run fast and he was good at tackling. 3

Personal response

Do you think Tom was brave?

Yes, because he tackled the man (does not say the man was big). 2

Response Key: 3 = Excellent 2 = Average 1= Weak

Word Detective

Phonics (0 – 1)

Phonic Assessment: Blending three phonemes

Page 8: Sound out the three phonemes (sounds) in 'ran'. Can you blend them? 0

Page 9: Sound out the three phonemes (sounds) in 'got'. Can you blend them? 1

Page 10: Sound out the three phonemes (sounds) in 'job'. Can you blend them? 1

Response Key: 0 = No 1 = Yes

Super Speller

Spelling (0 – 1)

Can you spell these words from memory?

Word	Pupil's spelling	Spelling (0 – 1)
you	*you*	0
stop	*stop*	1
saw	*saw*	1

Response Key: 0 = No 1 = Yes

Reading Level

Accuracy rate = 90 % Comprehension, Phonics and Spelling score = 12 /15

What Next?

5 miscues or fewer and 7+ for comprehension – move to next *Rapid* level.

If pupil scores below this – continue at this *Rapid* level and consider the following:

Michael is ready for Stage 2 Set B.

Problem	**Solution**
Some sight words not recognised	Use Writing PCMs for further practice
Hesitant and robotic reading	Demonstrate reading with pace and intonation
	Use 'Read and Record' feature on *Rapid Reading Assistant* Software
Comprehension weak	Paired reading of texts and encourage discussion
	Listen to 'Read to Me' feature on *Rapid Reading Assistant* Software
Phonic knowledge uncertain	Use Phonics PCMs for further practice
Spelling inaccurate	Further practice with 'Look Say Cover Write Check'

Rapid Running Record

Name: ______________________ Date: ____________

Story: Back at School RW = 50

Page	*Shaded words are not assessed*	Strategies used	Words assessed • = miscues
4	"I liked it when Sneaky Pete hid from Mr Cross," said a boy.		I liked it hid said a the children looked cross took cap sat on did you like at
5	"Ha! Ha! Ha!" said the children. Mr Cross looked cross.		
6	"I liked it when Cheeky Charlie took Mr Cross's cap," said a girl.		
7	"Ha! Ha! Ha!" said the children. Mr Cross looked cross.		
8	"I liked it when Cheeky Charlie sat on Mr Cross's cap," said a boy.		
9	"Ha! Ha! Ha!" said the children. Mr Cross looked cross.		
10	"What did you like best?" said the children.		
11	"I liked it when Nellie squirted water at you," said Mr Cross. "Ha! Ha! Ha!"		
12	The children looked cross.		

Key:
T = told O = omitted Sc = self-corrects
Strategies: Ph = phonic G = graphic S = syntactic C = contextual

Total miscues

Rapid Comprehension, Phonics and Spelling Record

Name:______________________ Date:______________

Story: Back at School

Text Detective

Questions to check understanding **Response (1 – 3)**

Literal recall
Where had Mr Cross and the children been? ☐

Inferential comprehension
Why were the children cross at the end of the story? ☐

Personal response
What would you have liked best about the trip to the zoo? ☐

Response Key: 3 = Excellent 2 = Average 1= Weak

Word Detective

Phonics (0 – 1)

Phonic Assessment: Initial letter sounds

Page 3: Find a word starting with the phoneme (sound) 'd'. (did) ☐

Page 7: Find a word starting with the phoneme (sound) 'ch'. (children) ☐

Page 8: Find a word starting with the phoneme (sound) 's'. (sat/said) ☐

Response Key: 0 = No 1 = Yes

Super Speller

Spelling (0 – 1)

Can you spell these words from memory?

the ☐
did ☐
like ☐

Response Key: 0 = No 1 = Yes

Reading Level

Accurate rate = ____ % Comprehension, Phonics and Spelling score = ____ /15

What Next?

5 miscues or fewer and 7+ for comprehension – move to next *Rapid* level.
If pupil scores below this – continue at this *Rapid* level and consider the following:

Problem	**Solution**
Some sight words not recognised	Use Writing PCMs for further practice
Hesitant and robotic reading	Demonstrate reading with pace and intonation Use 'Read and Record' feature on *Rapid Reading Assistant* Software
Comprehension weak	Paired reading of texts and encourage discussion Listen to 'Read to Me' feature on *Rapid Reading Assistant* Software
Phonic knowledge uncertain	Use Phonics PCMs for further practice
Spelling inaccurate	Further practice with 'Look Say Cover Write Check'

Rapid Running Record

Name:_______________________________ Date:_______________

Story: Tim, the Pest and the Ghost Train RW = 50

Page	*Shaded words are not assessed*	Strategies used	Words assessed • = miscues
18	"But I want to go on a ***big*** ride," said the Pest.		but I want
19	"Look!" said the Pest. "The Ghost Train is a big ride ***and*** I can go on it."		to go on
20	"But Ghost Trains are scary," said Tim. "But I ***want*** to go on it," said the Pest.		a big said the
21	Tim laughed at the scary ghosts and monsters. But the Pest did not laugh!		look is and
22	Tim said, "Let's go on the big Ghost Train again."		can it are
23	"NO!" said the Pest. "I want to go on the ***small*** rides."		at did not no

Key: T = told O = omitted Sc = self-corrects Strategies: Ph = phonic G = graphic S = syntactic C = contextual	Total miscues

Rapid Comprehension, Phonics and Spelling Record

Name: ______________________ Date: ______________

Story: Tim, the Pest and the Ghost Train

Text Detective

Questions to check understanding — **Response (1 – 3)**

Literal recall
Which big ride did the Pest want to go on? ☐

Inferential comprehension
Why did the Pest want to go on a small ride at the end of the story? ☐

Personal response
What kind of a ride would you like to go on? ☐

Response Key: 3 = Excellent 2 = Average 1= Weak

Word Detective

Phonics (0 – 1)

Phonic Assessment: Final letter sounds

Page 15: Find a word ending with the phoneme (sound) 'g'. (big) ☐

Page 17: Find a word ending with the phoneme (sound) 'n'. (can) ☐

Page 21: Find a word ending with the phoneme (sound) 't'. (not/Pest) ☐

Response Key: 0 = No 1 = Yes

Super Speller

Spelling (0 – 1)

Can you spell these words from memory?

had ☐
but ☐
are ☐

Response Key: 0 = No 1 = Yes

Reading Level

Accuracy rate = ____ % Comprehension, Phonics and Spelling score = ____ /15

What Next?

5 miscues or fewer and 7+ for comprehension – move to next *Rapid* level.
If pupil scores below this – continue at this *Rapid* level and consider the following:

Problem	Solution
Some sight words not recognised	Use Writing PCMs for further practice
Hesitant and robotic reading	Demonstrate reading with pace and intonation
	Use 'Read and Record' feature on *Rapid Reading Assistant* Software
Comprehension weak	Paired reading of texts and encourage discussion
	Listen to 'Read to Me' feature on *Rapid Reading Assistant* Software
Phonic knowledge uncertain	Use Phonics PCMs for further practice
Spelling inaccurate	Further practice with 'Look Say Cover Write Check'

Rapid Running Record

Name:______________________________ Date:________________

Story: Rugby Run RW = 50

Page	*Shaded words are not assessed*	Strategies used	Words assessed • = miscues
7	"I can stop him," said Tom. "No, Tom," said Kim. "The man is too big. You can't stop him."		I can stop him said no the man is too big you can't ran at but got he a saw good job
8	Tom ran at the robber. The robber ran fast, but Tom ran faster.		
9	Tom got the robber. "Got you!" he said. "Aaargh!" said the robber.		
10	A policeman saw Tom. "Good job, Tom," said the policeman. "I saw you stop the robber."		
11	"Good job, Tom," said Kim. "You got the robber. You can run fast."		
12	"Yes," said Tom. "I can run fast." "I *am* good at rugby!"		

Key:
T = told O = omitted Sc = self-corrects
Strategies: Ph = phonic G = graphic S = syntactic C = contextual

Total miscues [ ]

Rapid Comprehension, Phonics and Spelling Record

Name: ______________________ Date: ______________

Story: Rugby Run

Text Detective

Questions to check understanding — **Response (1 – 3)**

Literal recall
What did the robber steal from the lady? ☐

Inferential comprehension
Why did Tom say he was good at rugby? ☐

Personal response
Do you think Tom was brave? ☐

Response Key: 3 = Excellent 2 = Average 1= Weak

Word Detective

Phonics (0 – 1)

Phonic Assessment: Blending three phonemes

Page 8: Sound out the three phonemes (sounds) in 'ran'. Can you blend them? ☐

Page 9: Sound out the three phonemes (sounds) in 'got'. Can you blend them? ☐

Page 10: Sound out the three phonemes (sounds) in 'job'. Can you blend them? ☐

Response Key: 0 = No 1 = Yes

Super Speller

Spelling (0 – 1)

Can you spell these words from memory?

you ☐
stop ☐
saw ☐

Response Key: 0 = No 1 = Yes

Reading Level

Accuracy rate = ____ % Comprehension, Phonics and Spelling score = ____ /15

What Next?

5 miscues or fewer and 7+ for comprehension – move to next *Rapid* level.
If pupil scores below this – continue at this *Rapid* level and consider the following:

Problem	**Solution**
Some sight words not recognised	Use Writing PCMs for further practice
Hesitant and robotic reading	Demonstrate reading with pace and intonation Use 'Read and Record' feature on *Rapid Reading Assistant* Software
Comprehension weak	Paired reading of texts and encourage discussion Listen to 'Read to Me' feature on *Rapid Reading Assistant* Software
Phonic knowledge uncertain	Use Phonics PCMs for further practice
Spelling inaccurate	Further practice with 'Look Say Cover Write Check'

Rapid Running Record

Name: ______________________________ Date: ______________________

Story: Escape! RW = 50

Page	*Shaded words are not assessed*	Strategies used	Words assessed • = miscues
18	"Get me out!" said Sir Bold. Hal heard Sir Bold. "Where are you?" said Hal. "In the dungeon," said Sir Bold.		get out said are you I will must make a then think he ran at the into hid and was he could not
19	"I will get you out," said Hal. "You must trick Sir Crusher. Make a noise, then Sir Crusher will think you are getting out."		
20	"I will," said Sir Bold. He ran at the door.		
21	Sir Crusher heard the noise. He ran into the dungeon. Sir Bold hid behind the door.		
22	Sir Bold ran out and locked the door. Sir Crusher was cross. He could not get out.		
23	Hal and Sir Bold cheered and cheered. "You have tricked Sir Crusher," said Hal. "Now Sir Crusher is fed up!"		

Key:
T = told O = omitted Sc = self-corrects
Strategies: Ph = phonic G = graphic S = syntactic C = contextual

Total miscues: ______

Rapid Comprehension, Phonics and Spelling Record

Name: ______________________ Date: ______________

Story: Escape!

Text Detective

Questions to check understanding — **Response (1 – 3)**

Literal recall
Who helped Sir Bold to escape? ☐

Inferential comprehension
Who is the cleverer – Hal or Sir Bold? Why? ☐

Personal response
What do you think Sir Crusher will do next? ☐

Response Key: 3 = Excellent 2 = Average 1= Weak

Word Detective

Phonics (0 – 1)

Phonic Assessment: Blending three phonemes

Page 15: Sound out the three phonemes (sounds) in 'fed'. Can you blend them? ☐

Page 17: Sound out the three phonemes (sounds) in 'wish'. Can you blend them? ☐

Page 21: Sound out the three phonemes (sounds) in 'ran'. Can you blend them? ☐

Response Key: 0 = No 1 = Yes

Super Speller

Spelling (0 – 1)

Can you spell these words from memory?

here ☐
said ☐
into ☐

Response Key: 0 = No 1 = Yes

Reading Level

Accuracy rate = ____ % Comprehension, Phonics and Spelling score = ____ /15

What Next?

5 miscues or fewer and 7+ for comprehension – move to next *Rapid* level.
If pupil scores below this – continue at this *Rapid* level and consider the following:

Problem	Solution
Some sight words not recognised	Use Writing PCMs for further practice
Hesitant and robotic reading	Demonstrate reading with pace and intonation
	Use 'Read and Record' feature on *Rapid Reading Assistant* Software
Comprehension weak	Paired reading of texts and encourage discussion
	Listen to 'Read to Me' feature on *Rapid Reading Assistant* Software
Phonic knowledge uncertain	Use Phonics PCMs for further practice
Spelling inaccurate	Further practice with 'Look Say Cover Write Check'

Rapid Running Record

Name:________________________ Date:________________

Story: Jack's Dream RW = 100

<table>
<tr><th>Page</th><th>Shaded words are not assessed</th><th>Strategies used</th><th>Words assessed
• = miscues</th></tr>
<tr><td>3</td><td>I went to Africa.
POP! Out of my backpack came some binoculars.
I looked for fierce animals.</td><td rowspan="10"></td><td rowspan="10">I
went
to
out
of
my
came
some
looked
for
a
at
me
the
we
had
won
wanted
go
on
were
they
ran
away
then
up
was
he
said
but
came
see</td></tr>
<tr><td>4</td><td>A lion roared at me. I roared at the lion.
We had a fight. POW! I won!</td></tr>
<tr><td>5</td><td>I wanted to go to Planet Spot.
POP! Out of my backpack came a spaceship.</td></tr>
<tr><td>6</td><td>On Planet Spot were some aliens.
I roared at the aliens.
Zoom! They ran away.</td></tr>
<tr><td>7</td><td>I wanted to explore a wreck.
POP! Out of my backpack came a submarine.
I found a wreck.</td></tr>
<tr><td>8</td><td>I found a shark. We had a fight.
POW! I won!</td></tr>
<tr><td>9</td><td>I wanted to climb a mountain.
POP! Out of my backpack came a helicopter.
I zoomed to the mountain.</td></tr>
<tr><td>10</td><td>I found a Bigfoot. It roared at me.
I roared at the Bigfoot.
Zoom! The Bigfoot ran away.</td></tr>
<tr><td>11</td><td>Then Jack woke up.
"My dream was great," he said.
But then the lion, the aliens, the shark
and the Bigfoot came to see Jack!</td></tr>
<tr><td>12</td><td>Jack grabbed his backpack.
POP! Out of Jack's backpack came a motorbike.
Zoom! Jack zoomed away.</td></tr>
</table>

Key:					Total miscues
T = told	O = omitted	Sc = self-corrects			
Strategies:	Ph = phonic	G = graphic	S = syntactic	C = contextual	

Rapid Comprehension, Phonics and Spelling Record

Name: ______________________ Date: ______________

Story: Jack's Dream

Text Detective

Questions to check understanding **Response (1 – 3)**

Literal recall
What did Jack do when the lion roared at him? ☐

Inferential comprehension
Do you think Jack was really brave? ☐

Personal response
Would you be as brave as Jack was in his dream? ☐

Response Key: 3 = Excellent 2 = Average 1= Weak

Word Detective

Phonics (0 – 1)

Phonic Assessment: Initial consonant clusters

Page 5: Sound out the four phonemes (sounds) in 'Spot'. Blend the first two sounds. ☐

Page 11: Sound out the four phonemes (sounds) in 'dream'. Blend the first two sounds. ☐

Page 11: Sound out the four phonemes (sounds) in 'great'. Blend the first two sounds. ☐

Response Key: 0 = No 1 = Yes

Super Speller

Spelling (0 – 1)

Can you spell these words from memory?

out ☐
came ☐
wanted ☐

Response Key: 0 = No 1 = Yes

Reading Level

Accuracy rate = ____ % Comprehension, Phonics and Spelling score = ____ /15

What Next?

5 miscues or fewer and 7+ for comprehension – move to next *Rapid* level.
If pupil scores below this – continue at this *Rapid* level and consider the following:

Problem	Solution
Some sight words not recognised	Use Writing PCMs for further practice
Hesitant and robotic reading	Demonstrate reading with pace and intonation Use 'Read and Record' feature on *Rapid Reading Assistant* Software
Comprehension weak	Paired reading of texts and encourage discussion Listen to 'Read to Me' feature on *Rapid Reading Assistant* Software
Phonic knowledge uncertain	Use Phonics PCMs for further practice
Spelling inaccurate	Further practice with 'Look Say Cover Write Check'

Rapid Running Record

Name: ______________________________ Date: ______________

Story: The Treasure Tree RW = 100

<table>
<tr><th>Page</th><th>Shaded words are not assessed</th><th>Strategies used</th><th>Words assessed
• = miscues</th></tr>
<tr><td>16</td><td>Jim ran to see Captain Crab.
"Captain, Captain!" cried Jim.
"Let's climb that mountain!"<br>"What for?" said Captain Crab.</td><td rowspan="6"></td><td rowspan="6">ran
to
see
cried
let's
that
what
for
said
look
at
the
top
of
there
is
a
tree
you
can
and
get
we
grab
it
off
great
bad
come
on
lads
up
was
not
some
got
very
cross
how
far
now
then
this
but
where
all
no</td></tr>
<tr><td>17</td><td>"Look!" Jim cried. "At the top of
the mountain there is a treasure tree.
"You can see the treasure shining!
Let's climb the mountain and get the
treasure. We can grab it off the tree!"</td></tr>
<tr><td>18</td><td>"Great idea!" said Captain Crab.
"Bad idea," said Polly.
"Come on, lads," said Captain Crab.
"Let's climb up to the treasure tree!"</td></tr>
<tr><td>19</td><td>The pirates climbed up the mountain.
It was not easy.
Some of the pirates got very cross.</td></tr>
<tr><td>20</td><td>"How far to the top now, Jim?"
said Captain Crab.
"Not very far now!" said Jim.
"Then we can grab the
treasure off the tree!"</td></tr>
<tr><td>21</td><td>The pirates got to the top of the mountain.
"OK, Jim," said Captain Crab.
"This is the tree. But where is all the treasure?"<br>"Oh no!" cried Polly.</td></tr>
</table>

Key:
T = told O = omitted Sc = self-corrects
Strategies: Ph = phonic G = graphic S = syntactic C = contextual

Total miscues ☐

Rapid Comprehension, Phonics and Spelling Record

Name: ______________________ Date: ______________

Story: The Treasure Tree

Text Detective

Questions to check understanding **Response (1 – 3)**

Literal recall
Why did Pirate Jim tell Captain Crab to climb the mountain? ☐

Inferential comprehension
Why did Polly say "Bad idea"? ☐

Personal response
Would you have been cross with Pirate Jim? ☐

Response Key: 3 = Excellent 2 = Average 1= Weak

Word Detective

Phonics (0 – 1)

Phonic Assessment: Consonant clusters

Page 16: Sound out the four phonemes (sounds) in 'Crab'. Blend the first two sounds. ☐

Page 17: Sound out the four phonemes (sounds) in 'climb'. Blend the first two sounds. ☐

Page 18: Sound out the four phonemes (sounds) in 'Let's'. Blend the last two sounds. ☐

Response Key: 0 = No 1 = Yes

Super Speller

Spelling (0 – 1)

Can you spell these words from memory?

what ☐
very ☐
some ☐

Response Key: 0 = No 1 = Yes

Reading Level

Accuracy rate = ____ % Comprehension, Phonics and Spelling score = ____ /15

What Next?

5 miscues or fewer and 7+ for comprehension – move to next *Rapid* level.
If pupil scores below this – continue at this *Rapid* level and consider the following:

Problem	Solution
Some sight words not recognised	Use Writing PCMs for further practice
Hesitant and robotic reading	Demonstrate reading with pace and intonation
	Use 'Read and Record' feature on *Rapid Reading Assistant* Software
Comprehension weak	Paired reading of texts and encourage discussion
	Listen to 'Read to Me' feature on *Rapid Reading Assistant* Software
Phonic knowledge uncertain	Use Phonics PCMs for further practice
Spelling inaccurate	Further practice with 'Look Say Cover Write Check'

Name: ______________________ Date: ____________

My Reading Progress Chart

Stage 1 Set A

Key words
- ☐ I can read all 10 words on List 1A.

Phonics
- ☐ I can hear a phoneme at the beginning of a word.
- ☐ I can write the phoneme at the beginning of a word.

Comprehension
- ☐ I can remember what I have read.
- ☐ I can talk about what I have read.

Reading style
- ☐ I can pause when I see a full stop.

Stage 1 Set B

Key words
- ☐ I can read all 10 words on List 1B.

Phonics
- ☐ I can hear a phoneme at the end of a word.
- ☐ I know two letters can make one sound.

Comprehension
- ☐ I can remember what I have read.
- ☐ I can talk about what I have read.

Reading style
- ☐ I can pause when I see a full stop.

Stage 2 Set A

Key words
- ☐ I can read all 15 words on List 2A.

Phonics
- ☐ I can blend three-phoneme words.
- ☐ I can write some three-letter words.

Comprehension
- ☐ I can remember what I have read.
- ☐ I can answer questions about what I have read.

Reading style
- ☐ I always pause when I see a full stop.

Stage 2 Set B

Key words
- ☐ I can read all 15 words on List 2B.

Phonics
- ☐ I can hear the phoneme in the middle of a three-letter word.
- ☐ I can write most three-letter words.

Comprehension
- ☐ I can remember what I have read.
- ☐ I can answer questions about what I have read.

Reading style
- ☐ I always pause when I see a full stop.

Stage 3 Set A

Key words
- ☐ I can read all 20 words on List 3A.

Phonics
- ☐ I can blend two consonants at the beginning of a word.
- ☐ I can write some words which start with two consonants.

Comprehension
- ☐ I can guess what will happen at the end of a story.
- ☐ I can remember new facts from my reading.

Reading style
- ☐ I can change my voice for different characters.

Stage 3 Set B

Key words
- ☐ I can read all 20 words on List 3B.

Phonics
- ☐ I can blend two consonants at the end of a word.
- ☐ I can write some words which end with two consonants.

Comprehension
- ☐ I can guess what will happen at the end of a story.
- ☐ I can remember new facts from my reading.

Reading style
- ☐ I can change my voice for questions and exclamation marks.

Key word assessment: Stages 1–3

List 1A

at
in
is
it
on
and
had
did
yes
me

List 1B

he
go
to
the
got
but
can
will
was
not

List 2A

big
see
has
saw
his
said
with
him
like
here
you
stop
out
have
all

List 2B

are
very
down
must
our
some
want
went
came
they
this
get
that
old
into

List 3A

were
put
one
looked
for
away
off
wanted
lots
does
most
think
gave
then
fast
coming
jumped
would
now
open

List 3B

could
full
more
from
made
your
their
eat
again
so
where
took
what
live
home
who
her
there
just
half

Using *Rapid* at home

Stage 1

Sharing a book with your child will help them with their reading.

- First look at the *Before Reading* page together.
- Then look through the book and talk about the pictures.
- Take it in turn to read a page each.
- If your child gets stuck on a word, tell them the word.
- After reading, talk about the book together. What did you like best?
- Look at the *Quiz* page. Ask your child the *Text Detective* questions.
- Share the joke at the bottom of the *Quiz* page!
- Praise your child.

Stage 2

Sharing a book with your child will help them with their reading.

- First look at the *Before Reading* page together.
- Then read the first few pages to your child and ask them to read on.
- If your child gets stuck on a word, help them to work it out.
- After reading, talk about the book together. What did you like best?
- Look at the *Quiz* page. Ask your child the *Text Detective* questions.
- Share the joke at the bottom of the *Quiz* page!
- Praise your child.

Stage 3

Sharing a book with your child will help them with their reading.

- First look at the *Before Reading* page together.
- Then ask your child to read to you.
- If your child can't read a word, ask them to work it out. If they really get stuck, help them.
- After reading, talk about the book together. What did you like best?
- Look at the *Quiz* page. Ask your child the *Text Detective* questions.
- Share the joke at the bottom of the *Quiz* page!
- Praise your child.

BADGER MATHS
PROBLEM SOLVING
FOR YEARS 1-2

Mary Nathan

ILLUSTRATED BY JULIET BREESE

Contents

Introduction

Badger Problem Solving for Years 1-2 has been written to help develop the mathematical problem solving skills of children aged 5 to 7. The activities in this book support National Curriculum and Primary National Strategy objectives.

How the book is organised

The book is divided into five main sections. Each section focuses on a particular problem solving strategy and contains:

- an overview of the strategy and two detailed examples of problems that can be solved using that strategy;
- problems on photocopiable task cards, which children can work on independently or with teacher guidance as appropriate;
- teaching notes on each problem, together with answers and extension ideas for each activity.

There is a progression in strategies from using equipment and acting out a problem to recording results in a table. Similarly, the problems in a section increase in difficulty, and are aimed at Level 1, Level 2 or Level 3 of the National Curriculum. (The teaching examples are aimed at Level 2.)

There is one problem to a page, but there are usually several parts to an activity. Children could complete all the parts or only those that you select for them.

The last section in the book contains problems that could be used for end-of-year teacher assessment. A record sheet is included for you to track children's progress with the activities.

How the book relates to the Primary National Strategy and the National Curriculum

The chart on page 5 shows where each problem fits into a particular strand of the Primary National Strategy mathematics objectives. Most of the problems fit into the Using and applying mathematics strand, and references are given to main topic areas in other strands.

The activities address the Using and applying strand and the problem solving objectives in the National Curriculum for mathematics at Key Stage 1.

Using this book

You can use the book in several ways:

- to teach particular strategies and approaches for solving problems;
- when focusing on objectives from a strand other than Using and applying, in order to provide opportunities to practise skills and apply understanding;
- for homework;
- for preparation for end-of-year assessment;
- as assessment activities.

Generally, children are not required to record on the task cards. However, for some activities (particularly those in Using tables), it would be helpful for children to have a copy that they can write on. You may wish to work through a problem with a small group of children. Particularly with younger or less confident children, this approach would enable you to gauge their current levels of understanding.

Problem Solving

The Problem Solving Process

To help children tackle mathematical problems in a methodical way, it would be helpful to proceed through the following steps each time you start a new activity:

STEP 1: UNDERSTAND THE PROBLEM

- Encourage children to read the problem several times (or ask you to read it again) to make sure that they understand what it is asking.
- Children could underline or jot down pieces of information that they think are particularly important.

STEP 2: MAKE A PLAN

- Remind children of the different strategies that they know about, and help them to decide what sort of problem they are dealing with and which strategy would be most appropriate.
- At this stage, children should also be making estimates or predictions as to the outcome. This will help them to check whether their answers are correct.

STEP 3: SOLVE THE PROBLEM

- Children should always record their ideas and their methods. This will enable them to check their work more thoroughly, and also help someone else to work out what they mean.
- Encourage children to be systematic and to think about ways that they can organise their answers.
- Ask children to explain what they have done so far, particularly if they are stuck.

STEP 4: REFLECT

- Children should always check their answers and consider whether a solution makes sense.
- Discuss the methods that children used and help them to decide whether their method or someone else's was most efficient and why.

Copymaster

Name:

★ **Understand the problem**

What do you know?

. . . .

. . . .

What do you need to find out?

. . . .

. . . .

★ **Make a plan**

. . . .

. . . .

. . . .

★ **Solve the problem**

. . . .

. . . .

. . . .

. . . .

★ **Reflect**

. . . .

. . . .

. . . .

. . . .

Primary National Strategy (PNS) Links

PNS strand	Topic	Problem number
Using and applying mathematics	Real-life problems	3, 5, 6, 8, 11, 13, 16, 37, 44, A1, A4
	Patterns and relationships	1, 7, 10, 15, 16, 18, 21, 22, 24, 25, 26, 27, 28, 29, 30, 31, 32, 34, 40, 44, A2, A5, A7
	Presenting solutions	6, 7, 10, 11, 17, 19, 20, 21, 25, 26, 30, 31, 32, 34, 40, 41, 42, 44, 45, 47, 48, 49, 50, A3, A6
Counting and understanding number	Place value	23, 24, 36, 38, A5
	Comparing numbers	1, 3, 41, A1
	Fractions	6, 35
Knowing and using number facts	Addition and subtraction	1, 5, 7, 9, 16, 22, 25, 26, 30, 31, 33, 34, 37, 38, 40, 42, 43, 44, 47, 48, 49, A4
	Doubling and halving	3, 9, 28, 30, 33, 34, 36, 45, 49, 50, A3
	Multiplication and division	8, 12, 28, 29, 49, 50
Calculating	Addition and subtraction	1, 5, 7, 9, 16, 22, 25, 28, 30, 33, 37, 38, 43, 44, 45, 46, 47, 48, A5
	Multiplication and division	8, 12, 28, 29, 30, 49, A6
Understanding shape	Shapes	4, 10, 11, 18, 21, 27, 35, A2, A3, A7
	Turning and symmetry	17, 29, 39
	Position	13, 14, 15, 17
Measuring	Measuring	2, 9, 19, 20
Handling data	Recording data in lists and tables	20, 41, 42, 43, 44, 45, 46, 47, 48, 49, 50, A4

Using equipment and acting out

Teaching Notes

Using equipment and acting out

Many shape and number problems, like example 1 below, are set in contexts that involve equipment, and children should try to recreate the situations posed in the questions. However, providing opportunities for children to act out a problem that doesn't mention mathematical equipment, or asking them to model it, can help children understand better what is happening in that type of problem too, as in example 2, below. The equipment used does not always have to be maths equipment, and children can use all sorts of everyday objects to represent the different parts of a problem, e.g. books, pencils, crayons.

TEACHING EXAMPLE 1

You have four identical squares. You can lay them side-to-side. Sides have to touch all the way along their length. How many different shapes can you make from the four squares?

Understand the problem

What do we know?

4 identical squares.
Sides have to touch all the way along their length.
Shapes have to be different.

What do we need to find out?

How many shapes with different numbers of sides can we make?

Make a plan

What we did

Give children squares of paper or square tiles. They should keep the different shapes that they make so that they can see how many they have made. They should make these shapes.

Rectangle Square Hexagons Octagon

We can make five different shapes from four identical squares.

Reflect

Because it was possible to turn the shapes around to compare them, children could see that some identical shapes looked different just because they were in different positions, e.g. these shapes are actually identical.

Support

Ask children to make different shapes from 3 squares. Sides do not have to touch all along their length.

Extension

Ask children to investigate what shapes they can make if the squares do not have to touch all along their length.

Using equipment and acting out

TEACHING EXAMPLE 2

At the zoo, basher birds eat 2 snails and 1 worm each every day, but simper birds only eat 1 snail and 1 worm each every day. The bird keeper puts out 12 snails and 8 worms. How many of each type of bird are there?

Understand the problem

What do we know?

Basher birds eat 2 snails and 1 worm each every day.
Simper birds eat 1 snail and 1 worm each every day.
Simper birds eat the same number of snails as worms each day.
There are 12 snails and 8 worms.

What do we need to find out?

How many basher birds and how many simper birds are there?

Make a plan

What we did

Show children how to make worms and snails out of Plasticine (a simple ball would do for a snail), and ask them to make the 12 snails and 8 worms that the bird keeper had. They can then try different groupings of snails and worms eaten by each bird to try to find the right number. Ask:

- Are there only basher birds? (No, there are too many worms – only 6 would be needed if they were all basher birds.)
- Are there only simper birds? (No, there are too many snails – only 8 would be needed if there were only simper birds.)

Encourage children to try particular numbers of basher birds. They can then see whether what is left will feed simper birds (children should realise that they need to have an equal number of snails and worms for the simper bird), e.g.

1 basher bird: 2 snails and 1 worm
leaves 10 snails and 7 worms
2 basher birds: 4 snails and 2 worms
leaves 8 snails and 6 worms

3 basher birds: 6 snails and 3 worms
leaves 6 snails and 5 worms
4 basher birds: 8 snails and 4 worms
leaves 4 snails and 4 worms
Equal number of snails and worms.

The answer is 4 basher birds and 4 simper birds.

Reflect

Using Plasticine to model the snails and worms made it easier to try out different numbers of basher and simper birds. Being able to move them around and group them made it clear how many different birds there were.

Support

Ask children to find out how many snails and worms are needed to feed 3 basher birds and 3 simper birds.

Extension

Ask children to use what they have learnt so far to find out how many different birds there are for 15 snails and 9 worms, and 24 snails and 16 worms.

Problem Solving Task Card

Using equipment and acting out 1

Problem 1 Staircase

Numbers 1 2 3

Level 1

This staircase is made from cubes.

- ★ How many steps are there?
- ★ How many cubes are there in the first step?
- ★ How any cubes are there in the second step?
- ★ How many cubes are there in the whole staircase?

You can only see part of this staircase.
It has 10 steps.

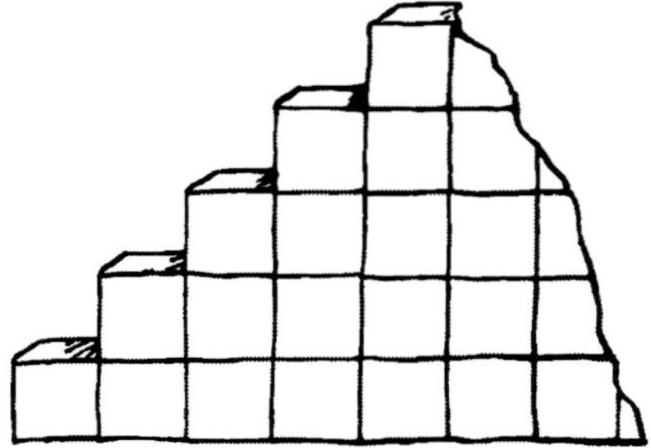

- ★ How many cubes are there in the seventh step?
- ★ How many cubes are there in the whole staircase?

Problem Solving Task Card

Using equipment and acting out 2

Problem 2

Measures

Level 1

Wonder worm

This is a baby wonder worm. It is 1 day old.

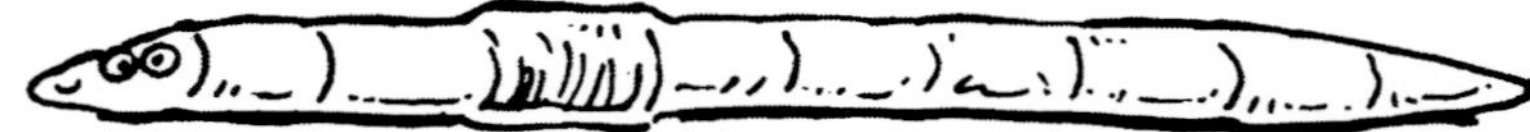

Each day the wonder worm is twice as long as it was the day before.

★ Make the baby wonder worm.

★ Make the wonder worm when it is 2 days old.

★ Make the wonder worm when it is 3 days old.

★ How old will the wonder worm be when it becomes longer than 1m?

PROBLEM 3 Numbers 123 Level 1

Birthday badges

The badges have fallen off these birthday cards.

★ Which badge belongs to which child?

Use these clues to help you.

- Ravi is older than Annie.
- Sara is younger than Li.
- Li is 7.
- Li is younger than Annie.

★ Ella is half the age of Ravi. Make a birthday badge for Ella.

★ Jason is twice as old as Sara. Make a birthday badge for Jason.

Shape & Space

Level 2

PROBLEM 4
Initials

Mark Newton's initials are M.N.

He can use counters to make his initials.

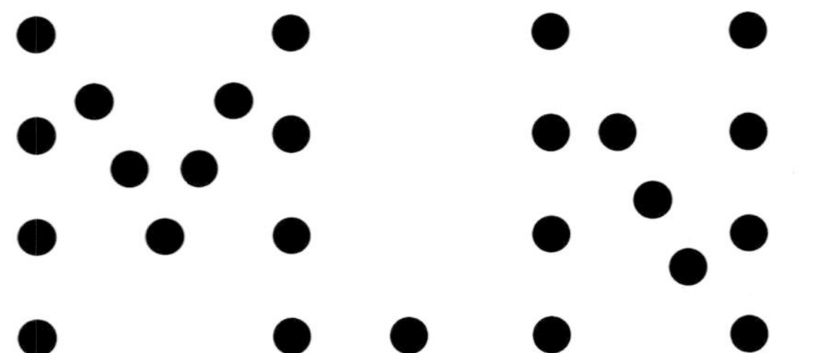

- ★ How many counters has he used?
- ★ What is the least number of counters he could use?
- ★ What are your initials?
- ★ What is the least number of counters you can use to make your initials?

(Don't forget the full stops!)

Mark has a middle name. It is Conor.

The initials for all his names are M. C. N.

- ★ What is the least number of counters he could use?
- ★ Ben has three initials. He used less than 30 counters. What might his initials be?

Problem Solving Task Card

Using equipment and acting out 5

Problem 5 — Slime

Numbers 123

Level 2

These are pots of slime.

You can mix the pots to make different colours of slime.

- Mix equal amounts of yellow and blue to make green.
- Mix equal amounts of red and blue to make purple.
- Mix equal amounts of yellow and red to make orange.

★ What different colours can you make?

★ You need 5 pots of yellow slime to make 1 large pot of orange slime. Can you make 1 large pot of orange slime using the pots above?

★ Use all the pots of slime. What colours do you make?

Problem Solving Task Card

Using equipment and acting out 6

Level 2

Problem 6

Numbers 123

Picnic panic

Class 2W are having a picnic.
The children have brought sandwiches.

Jane has brought jam sandwiches.

Tom has brought tomato sandwiches.

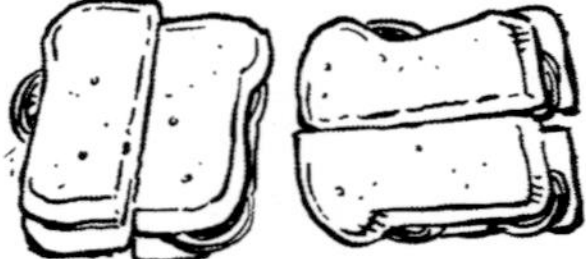

Charlie has brought cheese sandwiches.

Sally has brought salad sandwiches.

★ The children share the sandwiches so that each child has the same amount of each sandwich. What do they each receive?

Carrie has cucumber sandwiches.

★ Jane doesn't like cucumber.
How could the children share the sandwiches now?
(Remember: do not give cucumber sandwiches to Jane!)

Problem Solving Task Card

Using equipment and acting out 7

Level 2

PROBLEM 7

Numbers 123

Harold and the cabbages

Mrs Dazgupta had a rabbit called Harold.
On the day she went on holiday, there were 36 cabbages in her garden. When she came back, there were no cabbages left! Harold had just finished eating the last cabbage!

He ate one cabbage on the first day that Mrs Dazgupta was away. He ate two cabbages on the second day, three cabbages on the third day, and so on.

★ How many cabbages did Harold eat on the fourth day?

★ How many cabbages did Harold eat on the sixth day?

★ How many days was Mrs Dazgupta away for?

Each day, Harold had also eaten carrots. He had eaten two more carrots than cabbages each day. There were 100 carrots when Mrs Dazgupta went on holiday.

★ How many were left when she returned?

PROBLEM 8 Numbers 123 Level 3

Give a dog a bone

Twelve dogs stand in a circle.

Their owner gives every second dog a bone.

- ★ Which dogs get a bone?
- ★ Which dogs do not get a bone?

The owner gives every fifth dog a bone.

- ★ What happens?
- ★ What happens when the owner gives every fourth dog a bone?

- ★ When does every dog get a bone and when do only some dogs get a bone?

Problem Solving Task Card

Using equipment and acting out 9

PROBLEM 9

Numbers 1 2 3 | Measures

Level 3

Goldilocks' porridge

Goldilocks took porridge to the three bears.
Her pan held 24 cupfuls of porridge.

Baby Bear's bowl holds 1 cupful.

Mummy Bear's bowl holds 3 cupfuls.

Daddy Bear's bowl holds 4 cupfuls.

On the way, Goldilocks tripped over.
Three quarters of the porridge spilt out!

★ Was there enough porridge for all the bears to have full bowls?

★ How could Goldilocks have shared out the porridge?

(Remember: Daddy Bear gets the most.
Baby Bear gets the least.)

★ Baby Bear didn't want any porridge. How could Mummy Bear and Daddy Bear share the porridge?

Problem Solving Task Card

Using equipment and acting out 10

PROBLEM 10

Shape & Space

Level 3

Matchstick squares

This pattern is made from matchsticks.

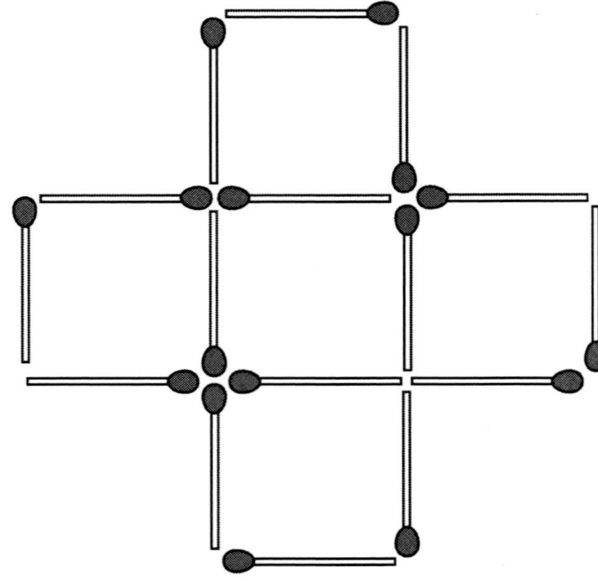

★ How many squares are in the pattern?

★ Make the pattern.

★ Move 3 matchsticks to make a different shape with 5 squares.

(Remember: all the squares must touch.)

★ Move 3 matchsticks to make a new shape with 5 squares.

★ How many different shapes with 5 squares can you make?

(Remember: you can only move 3 matchsticks at a time.)

Using equipment and acting out

PROBLEM 1 *Staircase*

Either show the diagram of the staircase to children or show them a model made from cubes. The first three questions give children an opportunity to understand the situation. Discuss the answers, asking children to say without counting how many cubes they think will be in the third and then the fourth step. Write the numbers of cubes in each step under the steps on the diagram. (1, 2, 3, 4, the number of cubes is the same as the step number.)

Ask the fourth question, and ask children how they can find the answer. Children are likely to count all the individual cubes. Some children might choose to add the numbers on the diagram. (10 cubes used in total.)

Show children the diagram of the second staircase, and pose the first question about it. Ask children what they could do to find the answer. What equipment could they use to help them? Encourage them to build a model of the staircase from cubes and, as they do so, ask them to predict how many cubes will be needed for each succeeding step. What do they notice about the number needed for each step? How many cubes do they think will be needed for the eighth / ninth / tenth step? (55 cubes needed for the whole staircase.)

Extension: Ask children to investigate the numbers of cubes needed for a 10-step staircase where each step is 2 cubes wide.

PROBLEM 2 *Wonder worm*

Children will need Plasticine and metre sticks for this activity. They each make a worm the same length as the worm on the page. Discuss how they can work out how long the worm is when it is 2 days old, and then ask them to try out their ideas. For the worm on Day 2 they make the worm twice as long (20cm), and then twice as long again for Day 3 (40cm).

Ask children to explain how they can find out how many days it will take the worm to grow to more than 1m. They might choose to put worms together to make the length of the worm after each new day. They should compare their worms with the metre stick. The worm will be 5 days old when it is longer than 1m. The worm will be 160cm, but children do not need to know the exact length – they only need to compare lengths with 1m.

Extension: Children can investigate how old the worm will be when it is as long as the classroom. They could do it with string, tape or strips of paper instead of Plasticine.

PROBLEM 3 *Birthday badges*

Children could act out this problem by taking it in turns to be the owners of the birthday cards. They could hold name badges as well as birthday badges. Children should make the connection between older and younger and larger and smaller numbers. You may want to discuss this first. The child acting as Li could stand on the 7 on a number line, and then other children could stand either side of them as their name is mentioned – a child older than Li stands to the right of him (as the class looks at them) on the number line and a child younger stands to the left. In this way, they should work out that Ravi is 10, Annie 9, Li 7, Sara 6. Ella is 5, Jason is 12.

Extension: The total of the ages of two children is 10. Make birthday badges for the children.

Using equipment and acting out

PROBLEM 4 *Initials*

Talk about initials and how they are formed. Ask children to make the initials in the diagram from counters and then to reduce the number used to find the least number needed.

Show how you would find the number for your initials by drawing your initials first and then placing counters on the top. Use as many counters as you want at first and then reduce them until only the minimum number is used.

Once children understand what they have to do, they can investigate their own initials. How could you use fewer counters to make your initials? Then ask them to investigate what initials Ben might have. Encourage them to investigate which letters require fewest counters to make them.

Extension: Ask children to make up a set of initials that uses exactly 20 counters. Children could start by finding sets of two initials and then sets of three initials that use 20 counters.

PROBLEM 5 *Slime*

This is an example of a question where maths equipment is not mentioned in the problem, but it can be used to help work out what the different options are. Children can use coloured cubes to represent the different colours of slime. Show how to pair a red and yellow cube together and say that this stands for orange slime.

Children can make orange (RY), purple (RB) or green (YB). To make a large pot of orange slime, children would need 5 pots of yellow and 5 pots of red. They don't have enough pots of red slime, so they cannot make a large pot of orange slime. If they use all the pots of slime, they can make 3 pots of orange (RY) and two pots of green (YB).

Extension: What could you make if you have 6 pots of yellow, 4 pots of red and 2 pots of blue

PROBLEM 6 *Picnic panic*

Give children paper shapes to match the sandwiches on the sheet. Discuss the fractions that each sandwich has been cut into. Children in groups of four could cut the paper shapes into the fractions shown, and then share them out. (Check that children understand that the tomato sandwiches have been cut into halves, and that the halves are the same even though they are facing in different directions.) The answer to the first question is:

 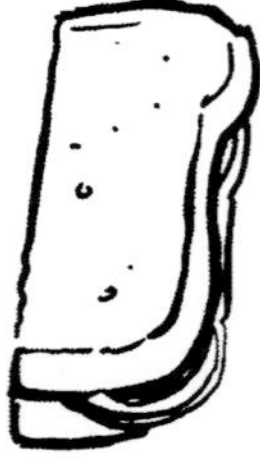 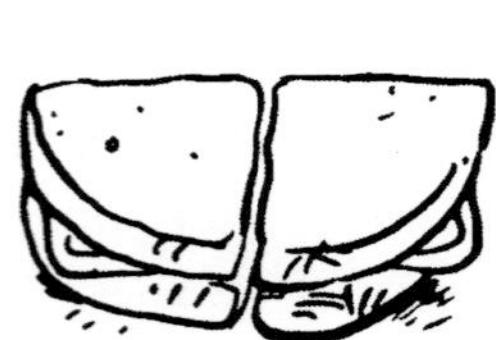 

For the second question, change the groups so that there are now five in each group and give out squares that could be cut into quarters as shown on the task card. Ask children to share the cucumber sandwiches out and find as many different ways as possible. How can they do it so that each child apart from Jane has a cucumber sandwich? Ask children to explain the different ways that they find.

Extension: Ask children to make their own type of sandwich and share it with their friends.

Using equipment and acting out

PROBLEM 7 *Harold and the cabbages*

Ask children to think about how they could use equipment to help them solve this problem. Children could put out 36 counters for the cabbages. Through answering the first two questions, they should realise that the total number of cabbages that Harold eats in a day is the same as the number of days that Mrs Dazgupta has been away.

He eats:

Day 1 1 cabbage
Day 2 2 cabbages
Day 3 3 cabbages
Day 4 4 cabbages
Day 5 5 cabbages
Day 6 6 cabbages
Day 7 7 cabbages
Day 8 8 cabbages

1 + 2 + 3 + 4 + 5 + 6 + 7 + 8 = 36
Mrs Dazgupta was away for 8 days.

Children could also use counters to work out the number of carrots that Harold ate. Higher attaining children might see that Harold ate 36 carrots plus 8 × 2 carrots.

48 carrots were left when Mrs Dazgupta returned.

Extension: Mrs Dazgupta planted cabbages to replace those that had been eaten. She planted 2 cabbages and 5 carrots each day. How many has she planted after one week?

PROBLEM 8 *Give a dog a bone*

This problem is an example of a number problem where using equipment to model the situation can help children to understand what is happening more easily. Demonstrate giving each dog a bone round the circle by placing a counter or a block on the dogs until you come to a dog that already has a bone. Ask children to say which dogs have bones and which have not. What do we call these numbers? (Even numbers get a bone, odd numbers do not.)

When the owner gives every fifth dog a bone, children should find that they count round and round the circle and eventually every dog gets a bone. But when they give every fourth dog a bone, only dogs 4, 8 and 12 get one.

Encourage children to try this for other numbers when answering the last question, e.g. for every third, sixth, seventh, eighth dog. They should notice that when the number is 3, 9 or even, then only some of the dogs get a bone, but when the number is odd and not 3 or 9, then all the dogs get a bone.

Extension: Children could investigate what happens for other numbers of dogs, e.g. 15 dogs, 11 dogs.

Using equipment and acting out

PROBLEM 9 *Goldilocks' porridge*

Children could use paper cups to stand for the number of cupfuls in Goldilocks' saucepan. They can try different methods to find what is left when three quarters of the porridge spills, e.g. halve the number of cups, and then halve what is left. They should find that they only have 6 cupfuls of porridge, which isn't enough for all the bears to have full bowls. (There must be 8 cupfuls for all the bears to have full bowls.)

If Baby Bear has porridge, children could share the 6 cupfuls in one way:
Baby Bear 1 cupful, Mummy Bear 2 cupfuls, Daddy Bear 3 cupfuls

If Baby Bear has no porridge, children could share the 6 cupfuls in two ways:
Mummy Bear 1 cupful, Daddy Bear 5 cupfuls
Mummy Bear 2 cupfuls, Daddy Bear 4 cupfuls

Extension: The next day, Goldilocks dropped a different porridge pan again. One fifth of the porridge spilt! This time there was just enough porridge for the bears to have a full bowl each. How much porridge was in the pan?

PROBLEM 10 *Matchstick squares*

Show children how to use matchsticks, pencils or lolly sticks to make the shape shown on the task card. Discuss which three matchsticks might be moved to make another shape, and then try out children's suggestions. Children can then move three matchsticks to make a different shape from five squares. They could draw the different shapes that they make so that they can compare the different shapes.

Discuss with children what makes one shape different from all the others that they have made so far (it cannot be 'turned into' another shape simply by turning it around or looking at it from another direction).

★ 3. These are the possible shapes that may be made:

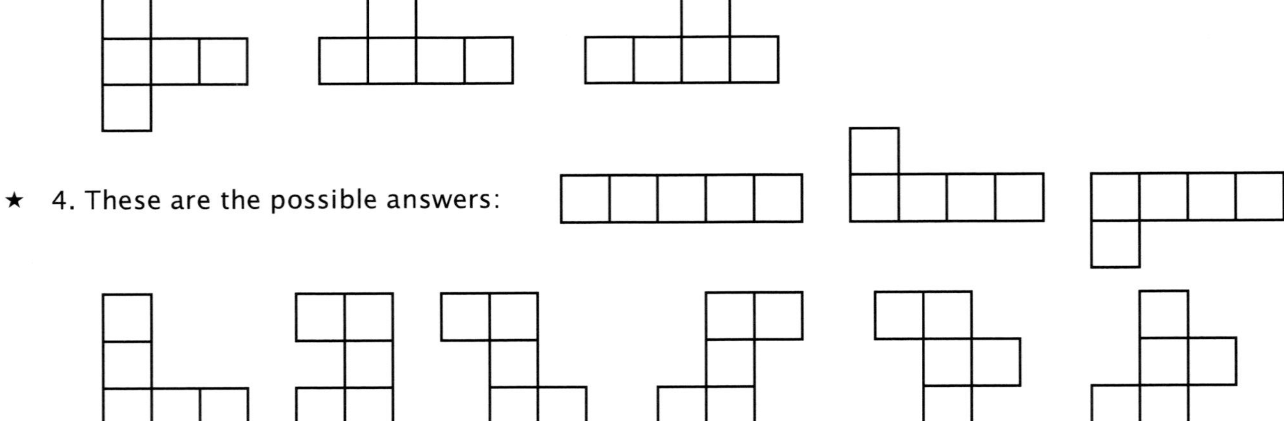

★ 4. These are the possible answers:

Extension: Can you make a shape from 5 triangles, where the triangles all touch? How many matchsticks do you use each time to make a new shape?

Drawing a picture

Solve
THAT PROBLEM!

Teaching Notes

Drawing a picture

Children will be used to making jottings when they calculate mentally. Drawing pictures and diagrams can also help them to visualise a situation, explore relationships, organise their ideas or record their solutions when they are solving problems. Some problems, like example 1 below, require children to draw a diagram when answering a question because they are about shapes. Children could solve others, like example 2 below, by drawing a diagram that helps them to work out what information in a problem means. These diagrams could be pictures of objects, number lines or mapping diagrams.

TEACHING EXAMPLE 1

What is the greatest number of times four straight lines can cross each other?

Understand the problem

What do we know?

We know we need 4 lines.

We know that the lines have to cross.

What do we need to find out?

How many times do the lines cross?

Make a plan

What we did

Children might begin this activity by simply drawing lines and then counting the number of crossing points. As children work, begin to ask them how they might increase the number of crossing points. Suggest that they start with two lines, then add a third and then add the fourth line, as below.

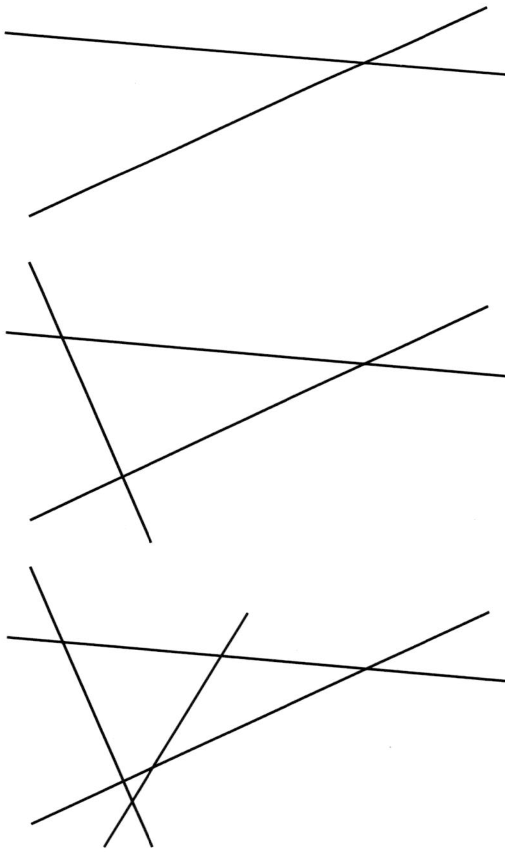

Children can then check their results by trying other sets of lines in other orientations.

Reflect

By repeating the investigation for several sets of lines, and comparing results with others, children should be able to begin to understand why the greatest number of times the lines can cross is 6.

There are 6 crossing points.

Support

Ask children to investigate three lines.

Extension

Ask children to investigate what happens with five lines. They could begin by predicting how many crossing points there will be, based on what they know about four lines.

Drawing a picture

TEACHING EXAMPLE 2

Sally used four different coloured blocks to build a tower. The yellow block was under the black block. The red block was next to the blue block. The black block was under the red block. Which block was at the bottom? Which block was at the top?

Understand the problem

What do we know?
The yellow block was under the black block.
The red block was next to the blue block.
The black block was under the red block.

What do we need to find out?
Which block doesn't have anything under it?
Which block doesn't have anything on top of it?

Make a plan

What we did
Children can decide which two blocks to start with and draw these in the middle of a piece of paper, e.g. 'The yellow block was under the black block.'

They can then look for any information about either of these two blocks. 'The black block was under the red block' means that the red block is on top of the black block.

Children then go through the final piece of information to decide where the blue block goes. 'The red block was next to the blue block' means that the blue block must be on top of the red block.

The blue block is on top and the yellow block is at the bottom.

		Blue
	Red	Red
Black	Black	Black
Yellow	Yellow	Yellow

Reflect

The information in the question was not complete; it did not say which block was on top or under every other block. Children have to take the information that they were given and work out what it also meant, e.g. when you already know that red is on top of black, then knowing that red is next to blue means that blue can only be on top of red.

Support

Ask children to solve a puzzle involving three blocks:
- red is on top of blue;
- yellow is under red.

Extension

Ask children to make up a problem for a friend to solve. They should try to conceal as much information as they can, while still leaving it possible for their friend to work out the answer.

PROBLEM 11
Classroom tables

These are the tables in three Year 2 classrooms.

Classroom 2N

Classroom 2R

Classroom 2G

There are 10 boys in each class.

There are 10 girls in each class.

★ Classroom 2N: Place the children so that no group of tables is empty.

★ Classroom 2R: Boys only want to sit next to boys. Place all the children so that no boy is sitting next to a girl.

★ Classroom 2G: Girls are not allowed to sit next to girls. Place all the children so that no girl is sitting next to a girl.

PROBLEM 12

Numbers 123

Level 1

Jugglers

Sam, Ben, Ian, Jo, Ali and Wu are jugglers.

They have a case of new juggling clubs.

★ On Mondays, the jugglers need 3 clubs each.
How many clubs do they need altogether?

★ On Wednesdays, the jugglers need 5 clubs each.
How many clubs do they need altogether?

There are 20 clubs in the case.

★ On Saturdays, the jugglers need 4 clubs each.
Are there enough clubs in the case?

Shape & Space

Level 1

PROBLEM 13
Rabbit runs

These rabbits have all dug burrows.

Each rabbit wants to visit each of his friends.
There must be a tunnel between each burrow.

★ How many tunnels will there be?

Another rabbit digs a burrow.

★ How many tunnels are needed now?

Problem Solving Task Card

Drawing a picture 14

Shape & Space

Level 2

PROBLEM 14
Super Baby

Super Baby likes to build towers.

Super Baby made a tower of 6 blocks.
He used the letters to make his name.

- A was beneath D.
- E was the second letter from the bottom.
- D was at the top.
- L was at the bottom.
- A was the letter above N.
- I was on top of E.

★ What order were the letters in?

★ What is Super Baby's name?

Level 2

Problem 15

Postman's walk

The postman delivers letters to these houses.

★ He delivers letters to each house. He only visits each house once. What could his route be? Find as many routes as you can.

★ The postman then delivers letters to these houses. He only visits each house once. What could his route be? Find as many routes as you can.

★ The postman visits these houses last. He visits each house only once. What could his route be? Find as many routes as you can.

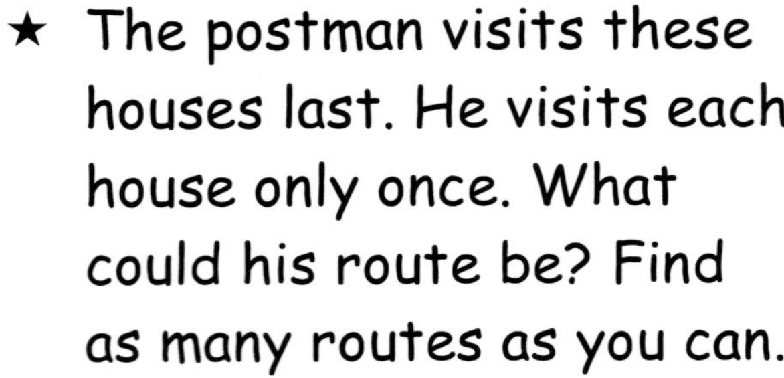

PROBLEM 16

Numbers 123

Level 2

Nut stores

A squirrel is burying some nuts under a tree. Each row, column and diagonal contains the same number of nuts. There is a different number of nuts in each place.

★ How many nuts should be buried in the empty places?

In the same way, the squirrel buries nuts under two other trees.

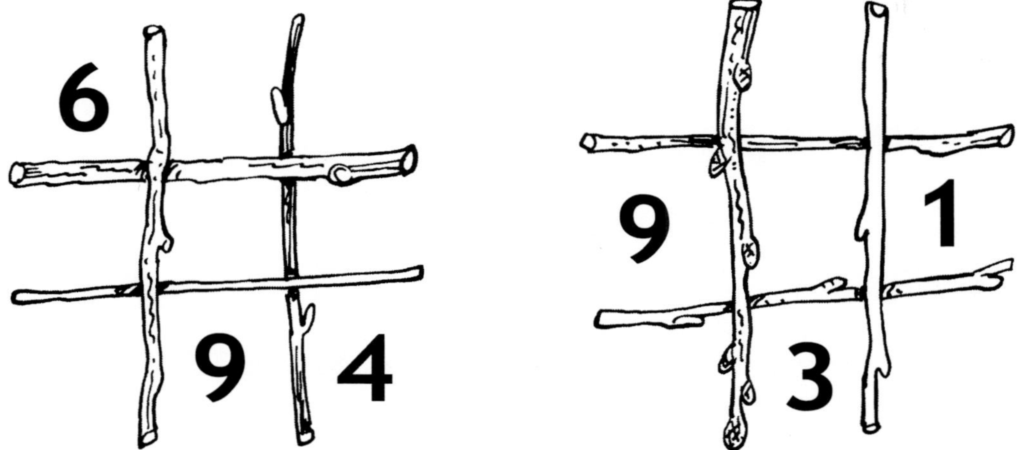

★ How many nuts should be buried in the empty places?

Problem 17

Shape & Space

Level 2

Snail trails

Selwyn is a snail. He likes long journeys. He never takes the shortest route.

★ Selwyn visited his friend Jim. Draw Selwyn's trail.

- Forward 6cm.
- Quarter turn anti-clockwise.
- Forward 5cm.
- Quarter turn anti-clockwise.
- Forward 5cm.
- Quarter turn clockwise.
- Forward 4cm.
- Quarter turn anti-clockwise.
- Forward 1cm.
- Jim's patch.

★ How far is it from Selwyn's home to Jim's?

★ Selwyn visited Grandma. Draw Selwyn's snail trail.

- Forward 4cm.
- Quarter turn clockwise.
- Forward 5cm.
- Quarter turn anti-clockwise.
- Forward 3cm.
- Half turn clockwise.
- Forward 7cm.
- Grandma's patch.

★ How far is it from Selwyn's home to Grandma's?

★ Selwyn goes for a walk. He only makes quarter turns clockwise. He only travels 5cm each time. Draw his trail. Where does he end up?

Problem Solving Task Card

Drawing a picture 18

PROBLEM 18

Shape & Space

Level 3

How many dots?

This is a square. It is made from dots.

You need 4 dots to show a square.

★ How many dots do you need to make a triangle?

★ How many dots do you need to make a pentagon?

★ How many dots do you need to make a hexagon?

★ How many dots do you need to make an octagon?

★ Use dots to draw two different pentagons, hexagons and octagons.

★ What do you notice about the number of dots you need each time?

Problem Solving Task Card

Drawing a picture 19

Level 3

PROBLEM 19

Measures

Home to the ant hill

The ants are going home at the end of the day.

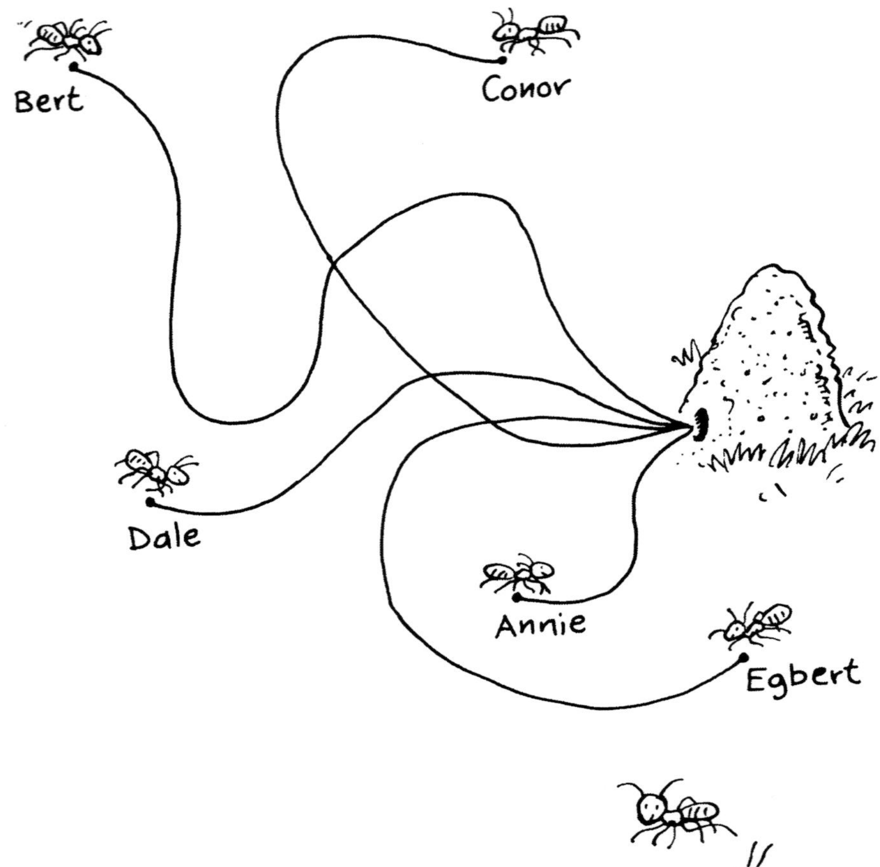

★ How far does each ant travel to get home to the ant hill?

★ Who travels the furthest?

★ Finola travels 18cm. Draw her journey.

★ Gary travels 7cm further than Finola. Draw his journey.

PROBLEM 20

Measures | Handling data | Level 3

Incy's weather

Incy Wincy Spider is climbing to the top of the drain pipe. The drain pipe is 20cm tall.

Every sunny day, Incy climbs 10cm.

When it rains, the rain washes Incy back 5cm.

This was the weather last week.

Sunday	
Monday	
Tuesday	
Wednesday	
Thursday	
Friday	
Saturday	

★ On what day did Incy reach the top of the drain pipe?

★ Where was Incy at the end of Saturday?

Drawing a picture

PROBLEM 11 *Classroom tables*

Begin by showing a small world model, e.g. a doll's house, to the children. Ask them to look down on it so that they see the furniture from above. Explain that the pictures at the top of the task card show the tables in a classroom from above. The lines beside the tables are the tops of chairs and they show where children can sit at a table. Talk about the first problem, and what it means. Ask children to explain what they are planning to do before they start. Children could then draw in circles for the children. Discuss the arrangements that children draw. Are they all the same? Why not?

Provide colouring pencils in different colours. Children can choose a colour for boys and a colour for girls. Read out the second problem and ask children to explain what it means and what they are going to do. When children finish, ask them to justify their solutions to the problem, and check that no boy is sitting next to a girl. Repeat for the last problem.

Extension: How could children sit in your classroom so that a boy always sits next to a girl? Draw a picture to show two different ways.

PROBLEM 12 *Jugglers*

Children can draw each of the jugglers. Then draw three clubs for each one and count them all. Ask them to tell you what their answer means, i.e. that the jugglers need 18 clubs for Mondays. Repeat for the other questions. Children should find that on Wednesdays the jugglers need 30 clubs. If there are 20 clubs in the case, there are not enough for the jugglers to have 4 each on Saturdays (there would need to be 24).

Extension: How many more clubs do they need for Wednesdays?

PROBLEM 13 *Rabbit runs*

Explain the problem, emphasising the fact that each rabbit has to be able to get from its burrow to all the other burrows. Children draw lines between the burrows. They should check that they have joined all the burrows together. They can then count all the lines that they have drawn. They should find that 6 tunnels are needed. For the next question, ask children first to predict how many burrows will be needed now. (10)

Extension: For a group of burrows, 15 tunnels are needed. How many burrows are there?

PROBLEM 14 *Super Baby*

As in example 2, children could choose the information about two letters and draw these in the middle of a piece of paper. They should then look for the information that relates to those blocks and build on from there. The blocks spell the name Daniel and D is at the top and L is at the bottom.

Extension: Use four of the blocks to make another word. Write a name in a puzzle for a friend to solve.

Drawing a picture

PROBLEM 15 *Postman's walk*

To avoid setting a limit to the numbers of routes that children find, give them dotted grid paper for them to use rather than giving them multiple photocopies of the diagrams on the sheet. When they have made several routes for one puzzle, ask them how they could sort their results into routes of particular types (e.g. routes with right angles only, routes with 'diagonals').

Examples of answers:

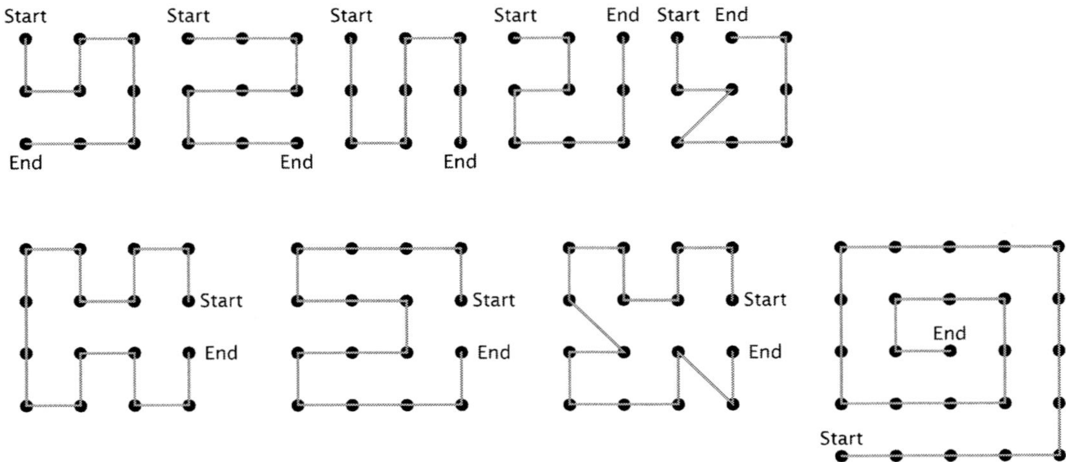

Extension: Find as many routes as you can for this group of houses.

• • • •
• • • • •
• • • • •
• • • • •
• • • •

PROBLEM 16 *Nut stores*

Discuss what is known about where the nuts are stored. Highlight that each row, column and diagonal has the same total. Children can draw grids of 9 squares to record their answers. They can total the middle column to find the total that they are aiming for and then use subtraction to find the other numbers of nuts. For the second and third groups, children already know the total of each row, column and diagonal, and so can use subtraction to find the missing numbers.

Answers:

4	9	2
3	5	7
8	1	6

6	1	8
7	5	3
2	9	4

2	7	6
9	5	1
4	3	8

Extension: Make up a puzzle for this set of hiding places.

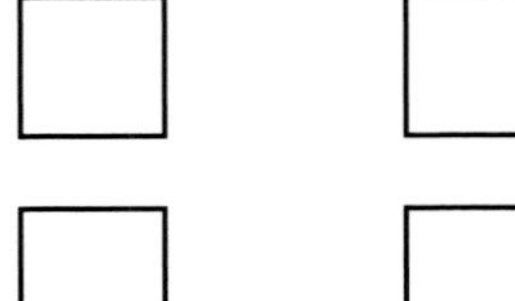

Drawing a picture

PROBLEM 17 *Snail trails*

Explain that snails leave sticky, shiny trails as they move around. Before children start the activity on the task card, they could practise the following routes in pairs: one child could be Selwyn and the other tells them the direction to move in. Provide centimetre square grid paper for children to record their trails on. They will also need rulers. Remind them to mark Selwyn's starting place on their trails as well as his destination.

Jim's home is 9cm from Selwyn's. Grandma's home is 5cm from Selwyn's. These are the trails Selwyn makes:

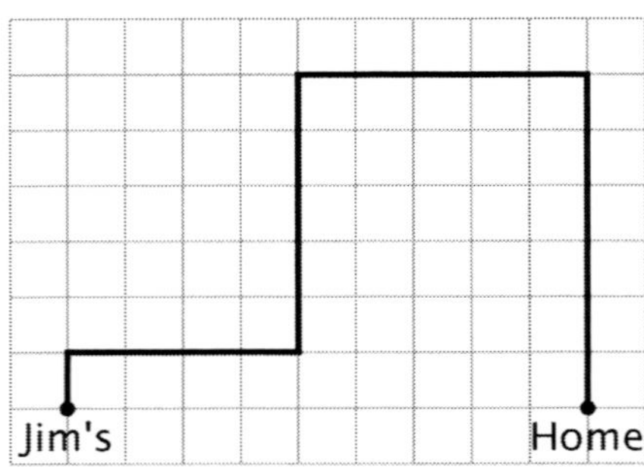

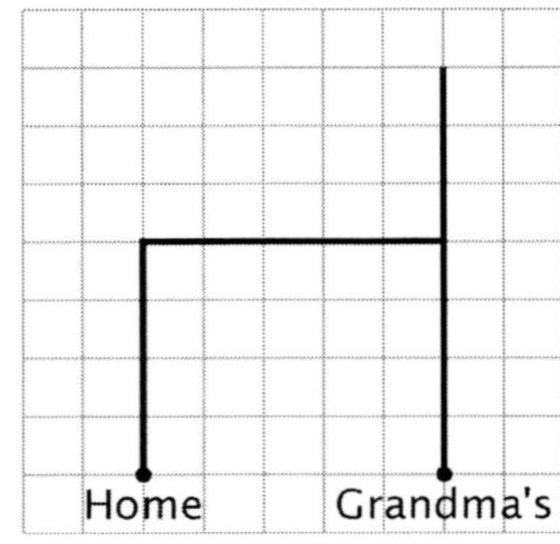

An example of Selwyn's walk is:

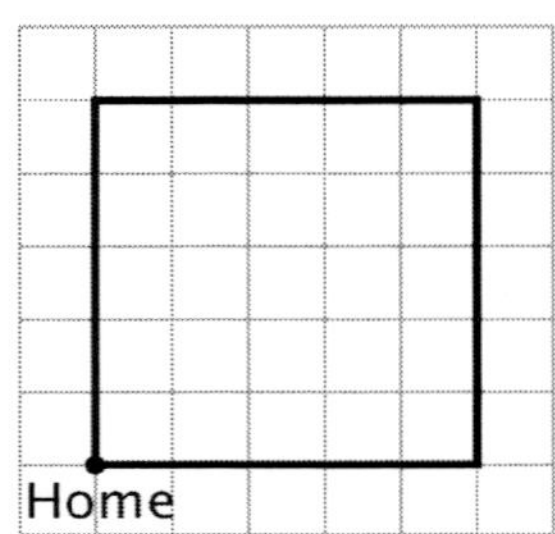

Extension: Selwyn went for a walk and came home. His whole journey is 20cm. What might his trail look like?

Drawing a picture

PROBLEM 18 *How many dots?*

Begin by showing children different 2-D shapes. Ask them to describe and name the shapes, giving their reasons as to how they know each shape's name. Explain that they only need 4 dots to show a square. Discuss why this might be so. Ask for suggestions about how many dots are needed for a triangle. Children can try the rest of the task card. They should begin to notice that they need the same number of dots as the number of corners the shape has.

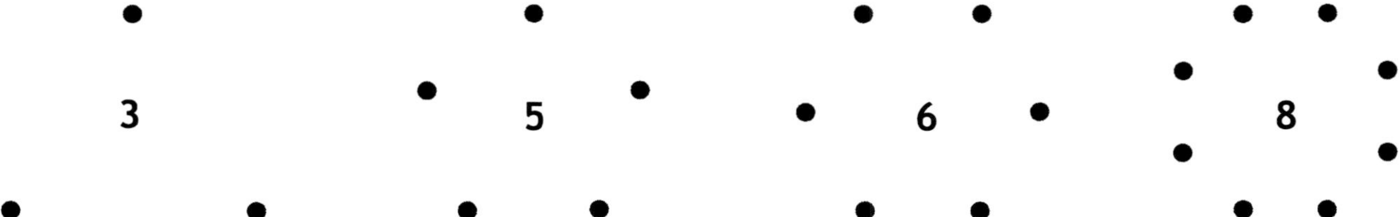

PROBLEM 19 *Home to the ant hill*

Provide children with a variety of measuring equipment, e.g. rulers, measuring tapes, trundle wheels, string, rulers. Group children in pairs or threes, and ask them to tackle the problems on the sheet. When most children have found one or two lengths, discuss the methods they are using and highlight the most efficient (laying string along the route and then measuring the string). Children should find these lengths: Annie 5cm, Bert 20cm, Conor 15cm, Dale 10cm, Egbert 15cm. Accept any lengths that are reasonably close to these. Gary's route should be 25cm.

PROBLEM 20 *Incy's weather*

Discuss the problem, and how drawing a picture of what is happening might help them. (They could use squared paper if that would help.) Encourage children to draw the pipe, and start with Incy at the bottom. They should draw what happens each day and write on how far up the pipe Incy must be.

Incy reaches the top on Thursday. On Saturday he is halfway up or down the pipe (at 10cm).

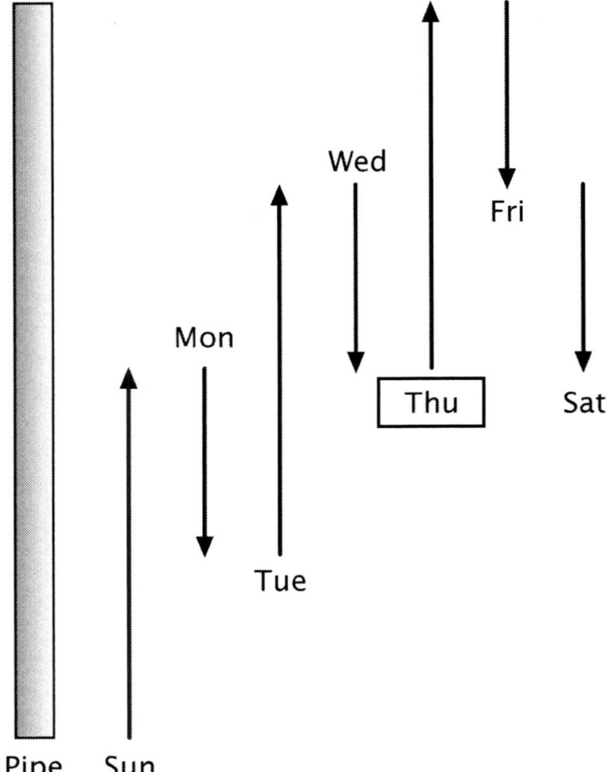

Finding rules and patterns, making predictions and checking

Solve
THAT PROBLEM!

Solve
THAT PROBLEM!

Teaching Notes

Finding rules and patterns

From an early age, children sort things by their similarities and differences, and looking for similarities and patterns is a very important skill when problem solving. In this section, children have the opportunity to develop this skill when dealing with both visual and number problems. They use their understanding of a pattern to help them predict what the next answer, number or shape might be. It is important that they then have the opportunity to check their predictions, because they should use what they find in the checking process to modify their understanding of the pattern. Therefore, making a prediction that turns out to be wrong can be as useful as making a prediction that was right.

TEACHING EXAMPLE 1

What number will be in the right-hand corner of the seventh row of this grid?

Understand the problem

1	2	3	4	5
6	7	8	9	10
11	12	13	14	15
16	17	18	19	20

What do we know?

The grid has the numbers 1 to 20 in it.
The grid has 5 columns and 4 rows.

What do we need to find out?

What is special about numbers in the right-hand box in a row?
How can we predict what that number will be in the seventh row?

Make a plan

1	2	3	4	5
6	7	8	9	10
11	12	13	14	15
16	17	18	19	20
21	22	23	24	25
26	27	28	29	30

What we did

Ask children to look at the numbers in the grid and to think about how the numbers change from row to row. Start by looking at 1. Some children might spot quite quickly that the number in the far right box is always a multiple of 5. Ask them to explain why this is. (There are five columns, so the fifth column is the last column and will always have a multiple of 5 in it.)

Ask children to predict what the far right number will be in the seventh row. Discuss the methods that children use to work this out, particularly the recording that they use. They can then add the next two rows to the grid, and check whether they were correct.

The number in the far right box of the seventh row is 35.

Reflect

By looking at the whole of the grid, it should be possible for children to find a pattern. It is important that they give themselves the time to compare numbers – this is how they will spot patterns.

1	2
3	4
5	6
7	8
9	10

Support

Children could investigate numbers in a grid like this and predict the numbers in the seventh row.

Extension

Ask children to predict what the number will be in the seventh row of this grid:

1	2	3	4	5
6	7	8	9	10
11	12	13	14	15
16	17	18	19	20
21	22	23	24	25

Finding rules and patterns

TEACHING EXAMPLE 2

How many squares will be in the tenth shape in this sequence?

Understand the problem

What do we know?

The first shape has 1 square.
The second shape has 3 squares.
The third shape has 5 squares.

What do we need to find out?

What will the tenth shape look like?
What is changing between each shape in the sequence?
What do we have to do to the third shape to make the fourth shape?
What do we have to do to the fourth shape to make the fifth shape?

Make a plan

What we did

Ask children to look at the shapes and to see what is different between them. They should soon spot that a square is being added to the front and the top of the shape each time. Ask them then to count the numbers of squares in each shape, and to look at the numbers: 1, 3, 5. Ask them whether the numbers are getting bigger or smaller, and by how much each time. Ask them to predict how many squares there will be in the next shape (7) and to justify their predictions. Invite a child to draw the next shape, and discuss whose predictions were correct and why.

Ask children to work out how many squares will be in the tenth shape, by adding 2 each time. When they have their predictions, children could then try drawing the rest of the sequence to see whether they were right.

The answer is 19.

Reflect

By looking at the shapes and looking at the numbers, children will come to understand the problem fully. They will also get a lot of satisfaction when their predictions prove to be correct.

Support

Children could investigate this sequence, and predict what the tenth shape will be.

Extension

Ask children to say what the tenth shape will be in this sequence.

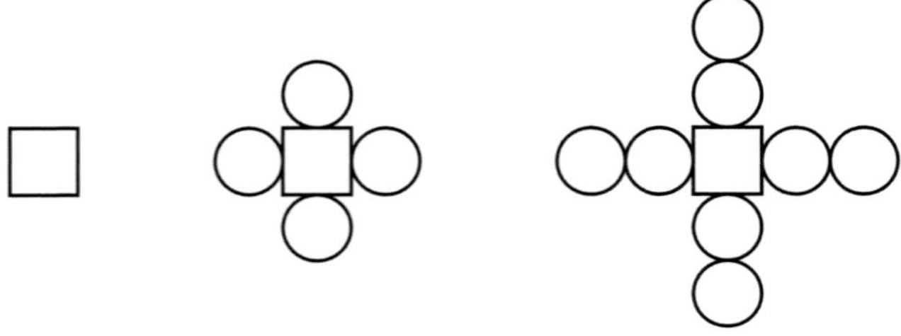

Problem Solving Task Card

Finding rules and patterns 21

PROBLEM 21

Shape & Space

Level 1

Necklaces

Sally's necklace has broken. She is mending it.

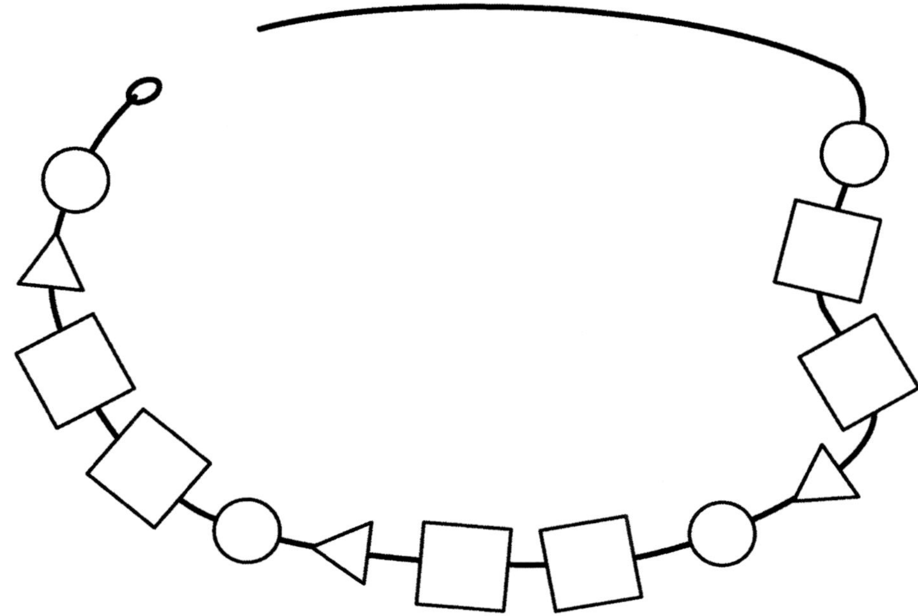

★ What shape bead comes next?

★ Draw the four beads that come after that one.

★ Ben makes a necklace. His beads are squares, triangles and circles. He uses 18 beads. Draw the necklace he could make.

(Remember: your beads must be in a pattern.)

★ Lily makes a necklace. She has 5 squares, 4 circles, 3 triangles and 2 rectangles. Draw the necklace she could make.

(Remember: your beads must be in a pattern.)

Level 1

PROBLEM 22

Numbers 123

The marble monster

The marble monster eats marbles.

On Monday, the monster ate 1 marble. 

On Tuesday, the monster ate 2 marbles. 

On Wednesday, the monster ate 3 marbles. 

On Thursday, the monster ate 4 marbles. 

★ How many marbles did the monster eat on Friday?

★ How many marbles did the monster eat altogether on Saturday and Sunday?

★ How many marbles did the monster eat all week?

Level 1

PROBLEM 23

Numbers 123

Digit duos

James picks two digit cards and makes a number.

★ What other numbers can James make with these digits?

★ How many numbers can he make?

Lauren picks two digit cards.

★ What numbers can she make with these digits?

★ How many numbers can she make?

★ How many numbers do you think Paul can make with his two digits? What are they?

★ These are your digit cards. How many numbers can you make?

Problem Solving Task Card

Finding rules and patterns

24

Level 2

PROBLEM 24 Numbers 123

100-square puzzle

This shape has fallen off a 100-square.

15	16	17		
		27		
		37	38	39

★ What do you notice about the numbers in the shape?

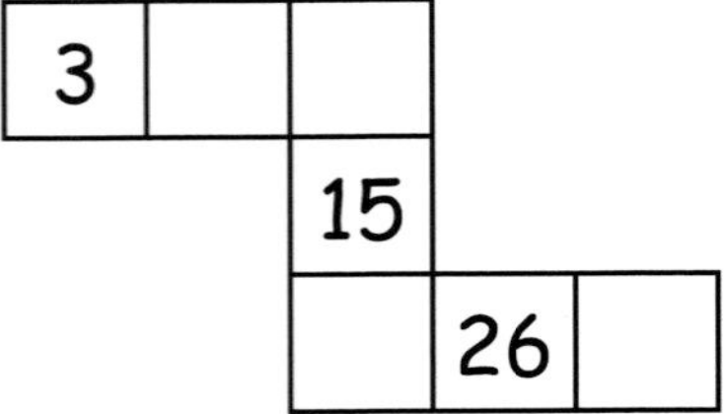

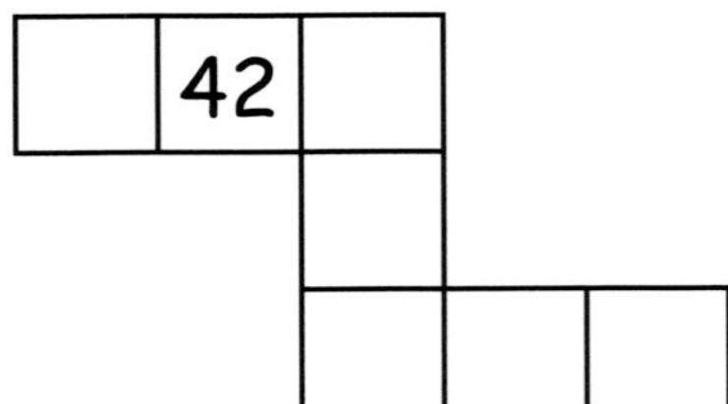

	6	

14

		24

★ What are the missing numbers in these shapes? How do you know?

Problem Solving Task Card

Finding rules and patterns 25

PROBLEM 25

Numbers 123

Level 2

New Year kisses

At New Year, Ben has to give everyone he lives with a kiss.

★ How many kisses does he give?

Everyone Ben lives with kisses him.

★ How many kisses does he receive?

★ How many kisses are given altogether?

★ Last year, Grandpa was away on holiday. How many kisses were given altogether without him?

Auntie Jasmine arrives.

She gives everyone two kisses. Everyone kisses her twice too.

★ How many kisses does Auntie Jasmine give and receive?

Level 2

PROBLEM 26

Numbers 123

Pyramid puzzles

This is a pyramid puzzle.

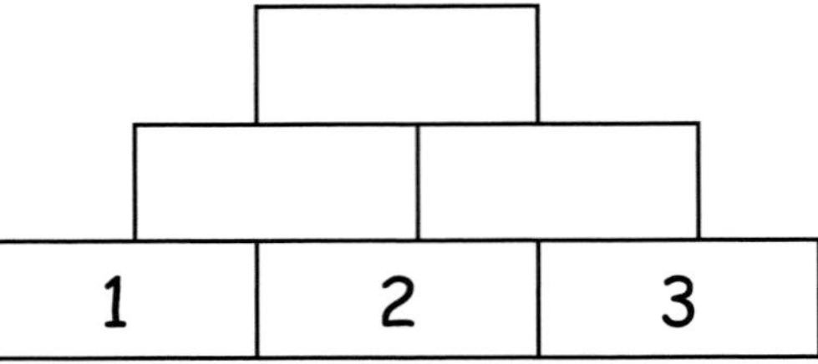

The number in an empty brick is the total of the two numbers in the bricks below it.

★ Complete the pyramid.

This pyramid also has the numbers 1, 2 and 3 in the bottom row.

★ What is the number at the top of the pyramid?

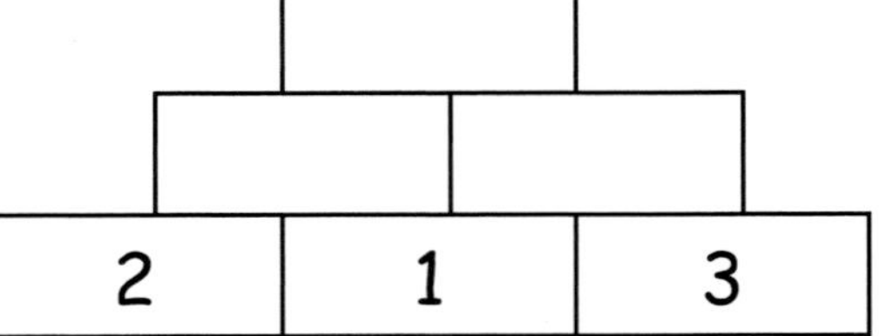

This pyramid also has the numbers 1, 2 and 3 in the bottom row.

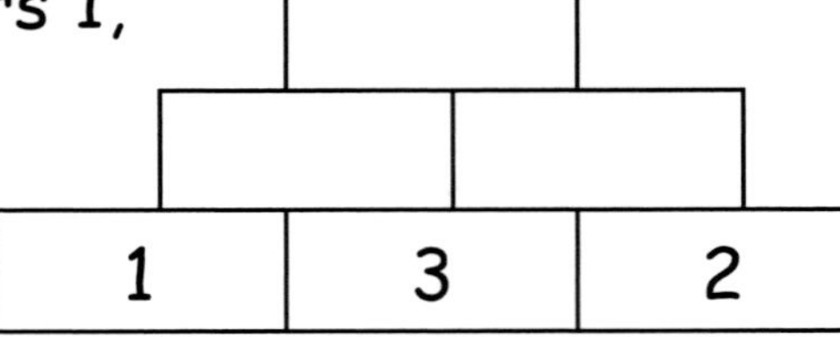

★ What is the number at the top of the pyramid?

★ What is different about these three pyramids? What is the same?

★ Choose your own three numbers. Draw three different pyramids. Try to get a different number in the top brick each time.

★ Try again for another set of three numbers.

Level 2

Numbers 123 | Shape & Space

Problem 27
Mr Blake's washing lines

Mr Blake's t-shirts have patterns on them.
What are the patterns?

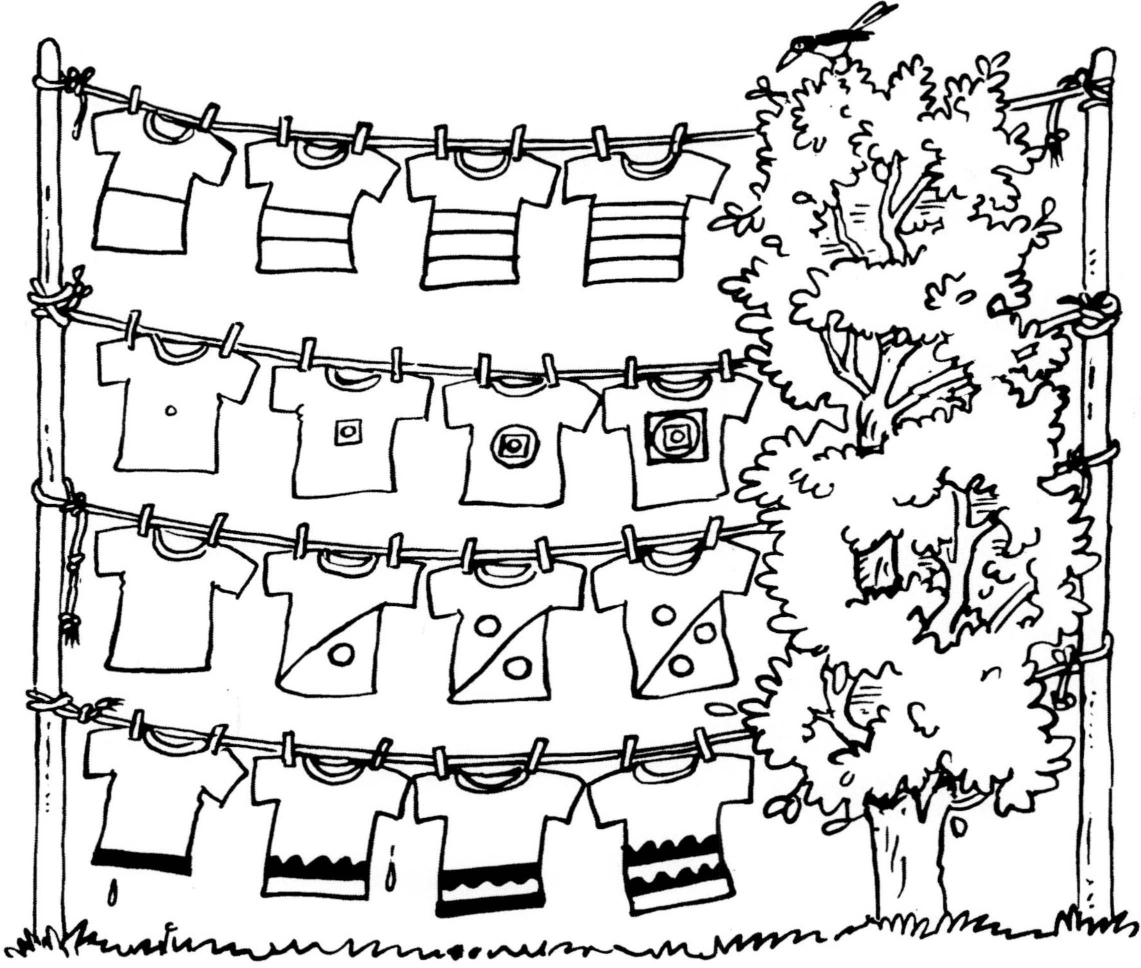

★ Draw the next two t-shirts on each line.

★ Draw two lines of t-shirts. Choose your own patterns.

Level 3

PROBLEM 28

Numbers 123

Triangle patterns

These are number triangles. They make a pattern.

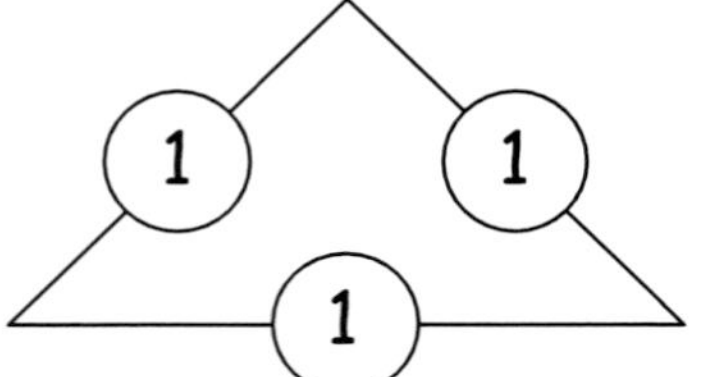

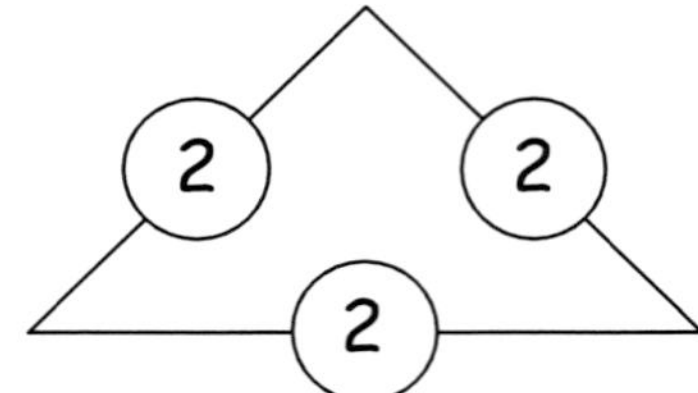

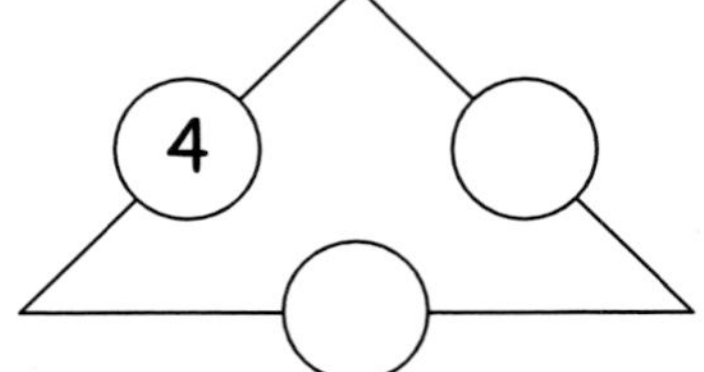

★ What are the missing numbers?
★ Draw the next triangle in the pattern.

These triangles make a pattern.

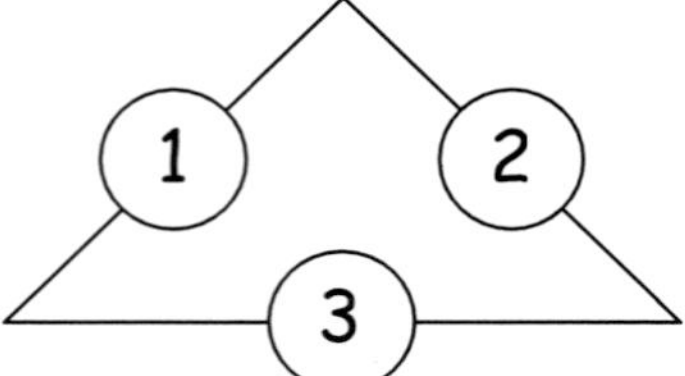

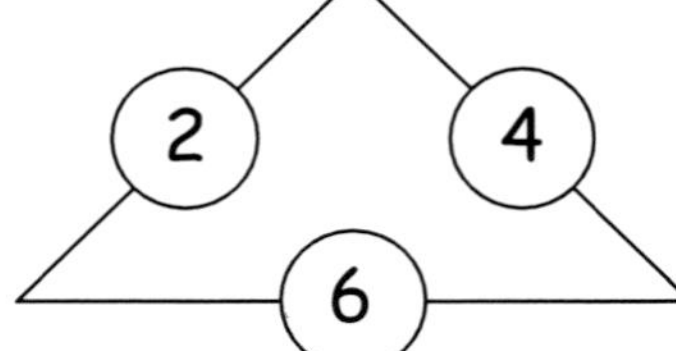

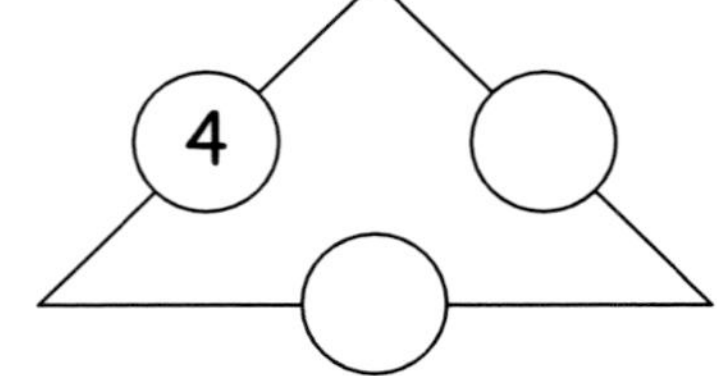

★ What are the missing numbers?
★ Draw the next triangle in the pattern.

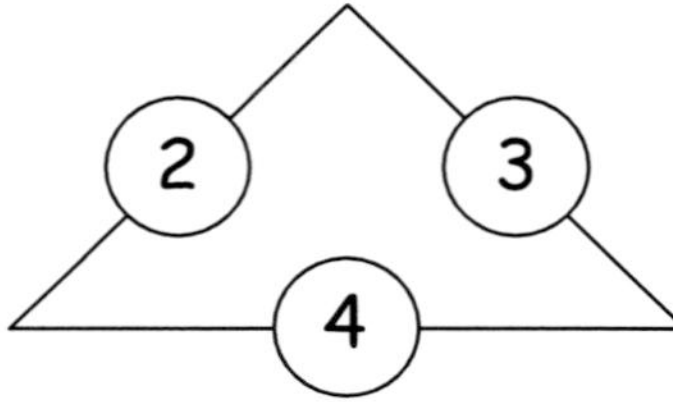

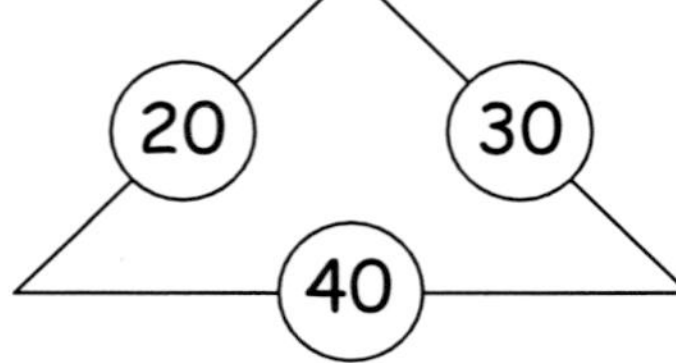

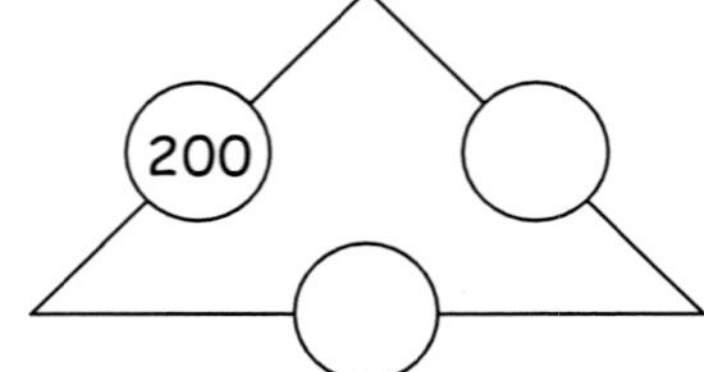

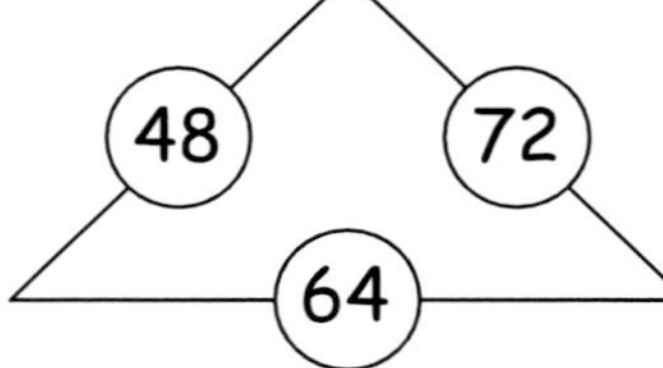

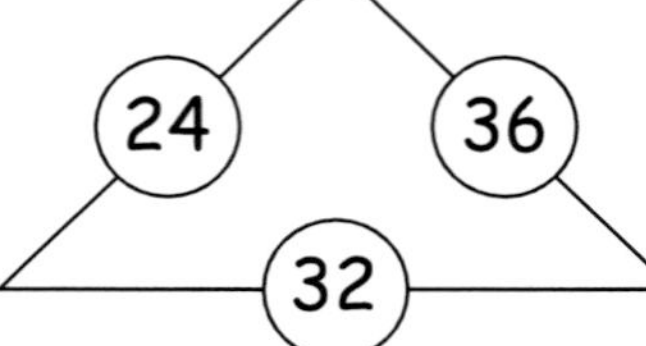

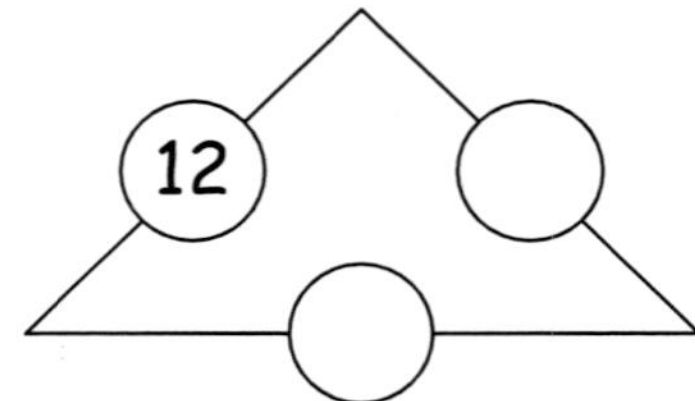

★ What are the missing numbers for these patterns?
★ Draw the next triangle for each.
★ Make up two triangle patterns of your own.

Shape & Space

Level 3

PROBLEM 29
Calculator digits

These are how digits are shown on a calculator.

0 1 2 3 4 5 6 7 8 9

★ How many right angles are in each digit?

This is a sequence of numbers.

9 99 999 9999

★ How many right angles are there in each number in the sequence?
★ How many right angles will be in the next number in the sequence?
★ What is the number?

This is a pattern of numbers.

4 44 444 4444

★ How many right angles are there in each number in the sequence?
★ How many right angles will be in the next number in the sequence?
★ What is the number?
★ Draw a sequence of numbers where the number of right angles increases by 1 each time.
★ Draw three different sequences where the number of right angles increases by 4 each time.

Problem Solving Task Card

Finding rules and patterns 30

PROBLEM 30

Numbers 123

Level 3

Charlie's choices

On Sunday, Charlie's aunt gave him some choices.

1 Charlie's aunt asked, "Would you like a penny on Monday, 2p on Tuesday, 4p on Wednesday, 8p on Thursday and so on to next Sunday, or would you like £10 now?" Charlie said, "I'll have £10 now please."

2 Charlie's aunt asked, "Would you like a penny on Monday, 2p on Tuesday, 4p on Wednesday, 8p on Thursday and so on for 10 days in total, or would you like £20 now?" Charlie said, "I'll have £20 now please."

3 Charlie's aunt asked, "Would you like a penny on Monday, 2p on Tuesday, 4p on Wednesday, 8p on Thursday and so on for a fortnight, or would you like £50 now?" Charlie said, "I'll have 1p today please."

★ Did Charlie make the right choice each time? How do you know?

Finding rules and patterns

PROBLEM 21 *Necklaces*

Begin by showing children different shapes and asking them to name the one that you hold up. Look out for any children who have difficulty recognising triangles and squares that are not sitting on a side. Invite them to rotate a triangle or a square so that they can see that it is the same shape whatever position it is in. Discuss the pattern made by the beads in the picture. Ask children to say what the pattern is (circle, triangle, square, square, circle, triangle...). Invite volunteers to explain how they know that the next shape will be a triangle and the four shapes after that two squares, a circle and a triangle.

Extension: Make a pattern for a bracelet. The pattern must go all the way round.

PROBLEM 22 *The marble monster*

Discuss the problem by asking children to put out the right number of marbles, counters or cubes for each day in the story. Ask them to think about the first question. What do they notice about the numbers of marbles that the monster is eating each day? What do they think the number will be on Friday? (5)

Ask children in pairs to say what they need to know to be able to answer the second question. How could they work this out? Invite children to suggest ways that they could check their answers. (The monster ate 6 on Saturday, 7 on Sunday: 13 in total.)

Encourage children to work in pairs to answer the last question. When children have worked out the answer (28 marbles), compare the methods that they used.

Extension: The monster's big sister eats footballs every day. On Monday she ate 2 footballs, on Tuesday she ate 4 footballs, on Wednesday she ate 6 footballs, and so on. How many footballs did she eat all week?

PROBLEM 23 *Digit duos*

Children could use digit cards to help them with this activity. Check that they say the numbers that they make correctly, and that they see why, say, 85 is different to 58. Discuss whether children should be allowed to include the digits themselves or only numbers that they can make by putting the digits together.

James	58, 85, (could also include 5, 8)	He can make 2 (or 4) numbers.
Lauren	16, 61 (could also include 1, 6)	She can make 2 (or 4) numbers.
Paul	29, 92 (could also include 2, 9)	He can make 2 (or 4) numbers.

They could only make one number (44) from the digits 4 and 4 (could also include 4).

Extension: How many numbers can you make from three different digit cards?

Finding rules and patterns

PROBLEM 24 *100-square puzzle*

Some children might need a 100-square to refer to when they start work on this problem. Discuss the patterns they notice in the numbers: numbers increase by 1 as they go from left to right; numbers increase by 10 downwards. Check that they use this understanding when finding the missing numbers for the other shapes. Ask them to justify the position of the numbers they find.

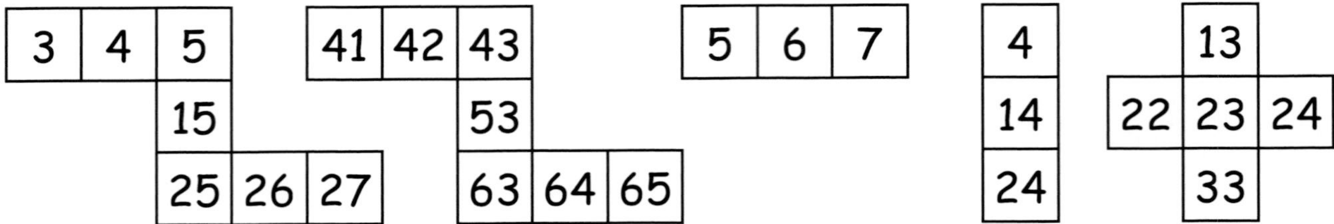

Extension: Make up a 100-square puzzle like this for a friend to solve.

PROBLEM 25 *New Year kisses*

When solving this problem, children should realise that each person kisses and receives kisses from four people (one less than the total number in the group). This means that the total number of kisses given is 5 × 4. Children could record their answer in different ways. Some might write out who kisses whom, and some might prefer to draw a diagram:

Ben kisses Grandma, Grandpa, Mum, Kate
Grandma kisses Ben, Grandpa, Mum, Kate
Grandpa kisses Ben, Grandma, Mum, Kate
Mum kisses Ben, Grandma, Grandpa, Kate
Kate kisses Ben, Grandma, Grandpa, Mum

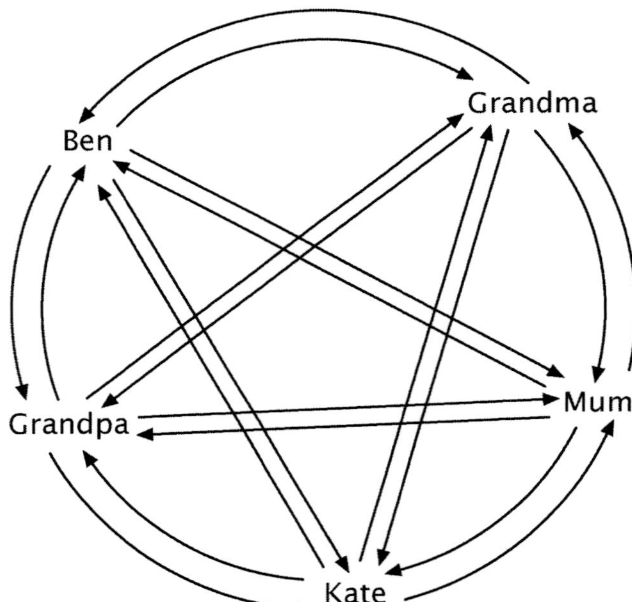

Ben gives 4 kisses and receives 16 = 20 kisses.

Encourage children to use this answer to help them predict what the number of kisses was when Grandpa was away. (4 × 3 = 12 kisses)

Aunt Jasmine kisses 5 people twice (5 × 2) and receives two kisses from 5 people (5 × 2). She gives and receives 20 kisses.

Extension: Next year Ben, Grandma, Grandpa, Mum, Kate, Aunt Jasmine and Uncle Sessay will be together. How many kisses will be given?

Finding rules and patterns

PROBLEM 26 *Pyramid puzzles*

Explain how the pyramids are created. In finding the missing numbers and creating their own pyramids, children will begin to notice that the position of the numbers in the bottom row affects the total at the top. The top number will be highest if the largest of the bottom three numbers is in the middle (because this is the position where the number is added twice).

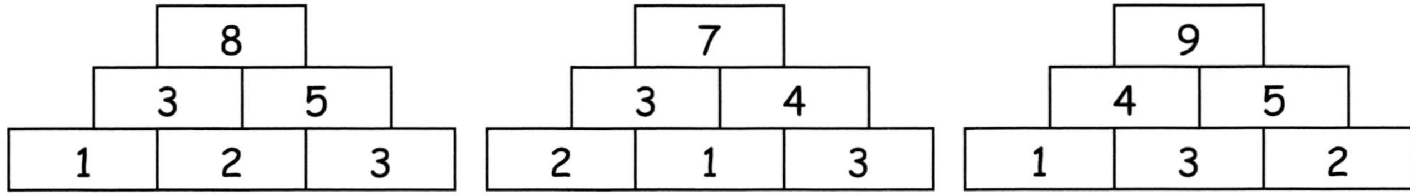

PROBLEM 27 *Mr Blake's washing lines*

In this problem, children have to work out what the visual repeating pattern is each time, and draw the next two elements in the sequences. Encourage children to talk to a partner about the patterns they have found, and ask them to justify the t-shirts that they have drawn.

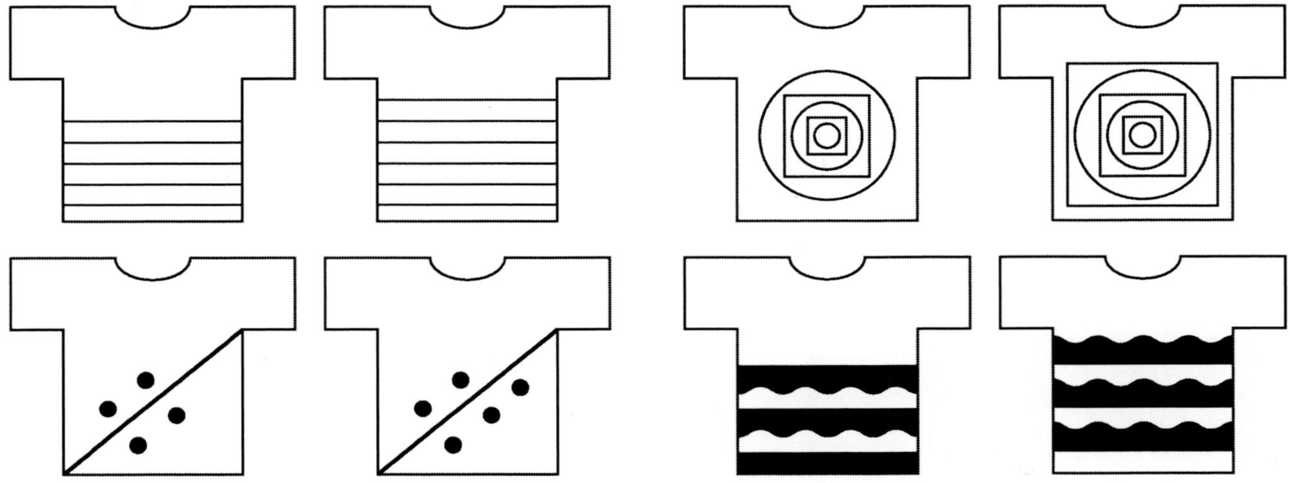

Extension: Draw a washing line of t-shirts that have a number pattern on them.

Finding rules and patterns

PROBLEM 28 *Triangle patterns*

Ask children to describe the differences between the two first triangles. What do they notice about the numbers? What has happened between the first and the second triangles? What do they think has happened between the second and the third triangles? Invite children to explain their reasoning. Repeat for the other triangle patterns.

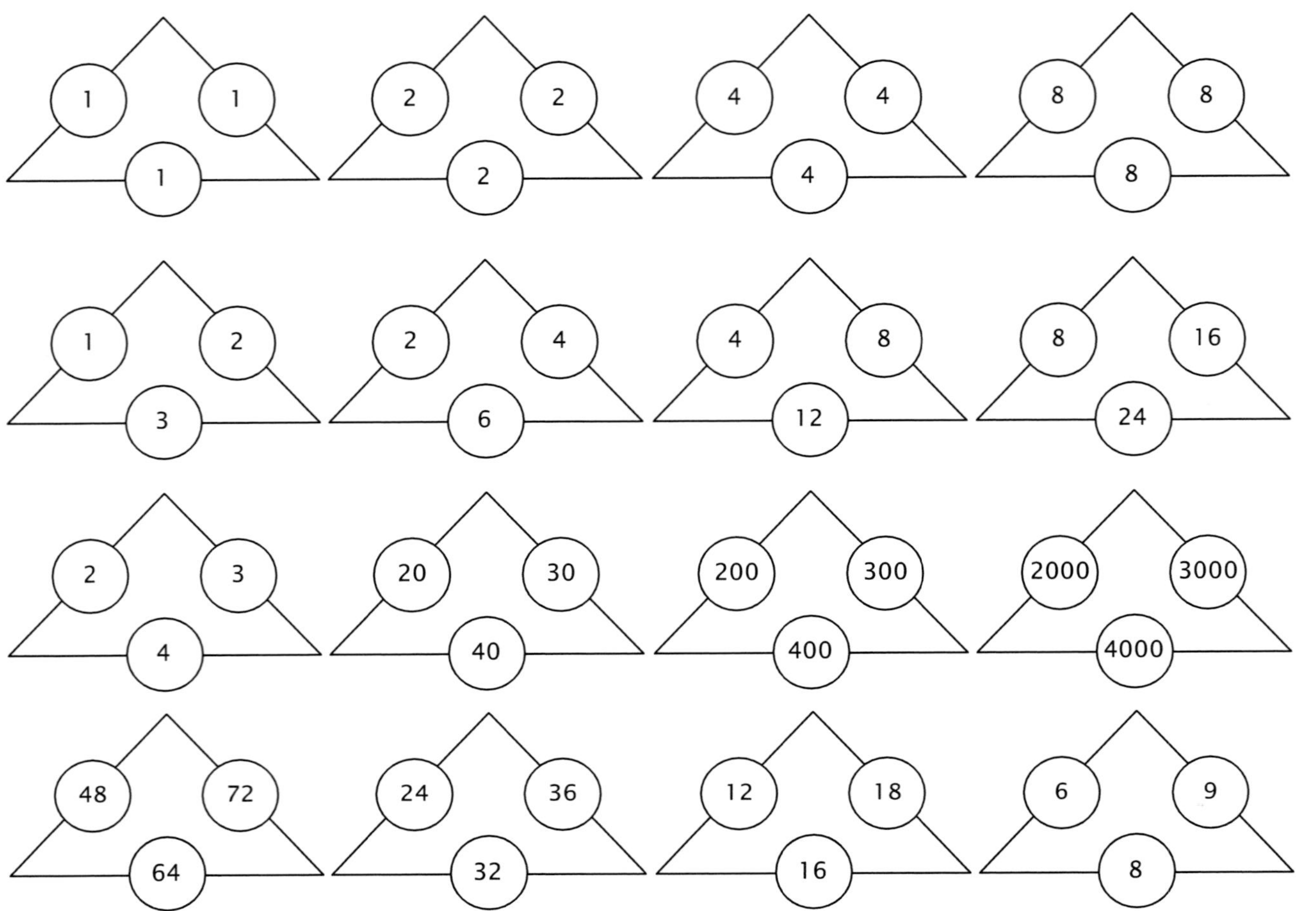

PROBLEM 29 *Calculator digits*

Before children start the activity, practise making quarter turns and look for right angles in shapes around the classroom. [Right-angles: 0 4, 1 0, 2 4, 3 4, 4 3, 5 4, 6 6, 7 1, 8 8, 9 5]

Ask children to explain what is happening in the first sequence. Highlight the fact that each new number in the sequence has one more digit that the previous number, and so it has 5 more right angles. There are 5, 10, 15, 20 right angles in the sequence. The next number will have 25 right angles and it is 99 999.

The second sequence has 3, 6, 9, 12 right angles in the numbers. The next number will have 15 right angles and it is 44 444.

The sequence that grows by 1 each time is based on 7. For sequences that grow by 4 right angles each time, children could draw numbers consisting of 2, 3 or 5.

Extension: Make a sequence that begins with a 2-digit number, e.g. 68.

Finding rules and patterns

PROBLEM 30 *Charlie's choices*

Provide children with calculators for the activity. Explain the choices that Charlie's aunt is giving him each time, and check that children understand each of the time scales. They could work in pairs to calculate the amount that Charlie would have at the end of each period. Ask them to explain the pattern of numbers that they are making, and consequently why Charlie made the choices that he did. Charlie made the right choice each time. This is the pattern of amounts:

Monday	1p
Tuesday	+ 2p
Wednesday	+ 4p
Thursday	+ 8p
Friday	+ 16p
Saturday	+ 32p
Sunday	+ 64p
	£1.27

(So £10 the previous Sunday was the right choice.)

Monday	+ £1.28
Tuesday	+ £2.56
Wednesday	+ £5.12
	£10.23

(So £20 the previous Sunday was the right choice.)

Thursday	+ £10.24
Friday	+ £20.48
Saturday	+ £40.96
Sunday	+ £81.92
	£163.83

(So receiving 1p 2 weeks before and doubling the amount received every day was the right choice.)

Extension: Make up a similar puzzle that starts with Charlie's aunt giving 2p to Charlie.

Finding all the possibilities

Solve
THAT PROBLEM!

Solve
THAT PROBLEM!

Solve
THAT PROBLEM!

Teaching Notes

Finding all the possibilities

Children often think of mathematics as a subject where there is just one answer. It is important, therefore, that they have opportunities to investigate mathematical situations that have several answers, and perhaps even an infinite number of answers. However, to enable them to make the most of these opportunities it is necessary to help them to learn to be methodical and organised in the way they generate results. Encouraging children to look at the sorts of answers they are getting will help them to think of new ways to find answers and so keep them motivated to continue until all the possibilities are found.

TEACHING EXAMPLE 1

Using your age, +, −, × , ÷ and =, how many numbers from 1 to 20 can you make?

Understand the problem

What do we know?
We know that we can use our age, +, −, × , ÷ and =.

What do we need to find out?
We have to find numbers from 1 to 20.
How do we make the numbers from 1 to 20?

Make a plan

What we did
Children could work in pairs for this activity. You might also like to give the numbers that are less than the children's age to the higher attaining children in the class. Children could begin by seeing which numbers they can make by adding their age to itself, e.g. 6 + 6 = 12, 12 + 6 = 18. They could then investigate what happens when they divide their age by itself, e.g. 6 ÷ 6 = 1. They could also use their answers to generate other numbers, e.g. 1 + 6 = 7, and so on. Tell children that they will have to explain to the rest of the class how they made a particular number, so they will have to keep a very clear record of what they did.

Check children's answers and invite pairs to look over what other pairs have done and compare methods. As a class, discuss children's methods. Which were the most efficient and quickest? Which took the longest? Which number facts did children use most often?

Reflect

Children will find that keeping clear jottings of the methods that they used will help them to present their results easily. They should also find that it helped them to see the numbers that they could use to generate other answers.

Support

Children could investigate how many numbers from 1 to 10 they can make with the numbers 1 and 2 and + and =.

Extension

Children could explore ways of using their age, doubling and halving and ×, ÷ and = to make the numbers from 1 to 10.

Finding all the possibilities

TEACHING EXAMPLE 2

How many different ways can you score 10 by rolling three dice?

Understand the problem

What do we know?
We know that we have three dice.
We know that we have to score 10.

What do we need to find out?
Which numbers do we have to score when we roll three dice?
Which numbers can we score from one dice?

Make a plan

What we did
Give dice out to pairs of children, and let them take it in turns to throw the dice several times and record their scores. Discuss the scores that it is possible to get from one dice. Ask children to say what the highest score would be from 3 dice (18) and the lowest score (3). Ask children to write 10 in the middle of their piece of paper and to write down as many ways as they can to make it using addition. After a minute, ask children to give some examples. Then ask them to think about the numbers that are on a dice. They then need to disregard any additions that involve 0 or any numbers greater than 6, as only numbers that appear on the dice can be included.

Ask children to return to generating their results. To help them keep going, ask them to organise their answers, e.g. put all the additions that begin with 1 together. When children have finished, discuss the results that they found, and ask them to write them on the board. Discuss the results that children have found, particularly those that have the same numbers in them, e.g. 1 + 3 + 6, 3 + 1 + 6 and 6 + 3 + 1. Are these the same or different? Why?

1 + 3 + 6 = 10
1 + 4 + 5 = 10
2 + 2 + 6 = 10
2 + 3 + 5 = 10
2 + 4 + 4 = 10
3 + 3 + 4 = 10

Reflect

Grouping results together will help children think of other possibilities they could try, e.g. if they are looking at several calculations that start with 1 but none of them includes a 4, they could try to make a calculation that does.

Support

Children could find all the ways to score 7 from two dice.

Extension

Children could investigate how many different ways there are to score 13 from three dice.

Problem 31

Numbers 123

Level 1

Toys

These toys have separate heads, bodies and legs.

★ How many different toys can you make from the two sets of parts?

PROBLEM 32

Numbers 123

Level 1

Bedtime

Pete has a rabbit, a cat and a dog.

Sometimes they like to sleep all together.

Sometimes they like to sleep on their own.

Sometimes they like to sleep in a pair and on their own.

★ How many different ways can they sleep?

Pete gets a snake.

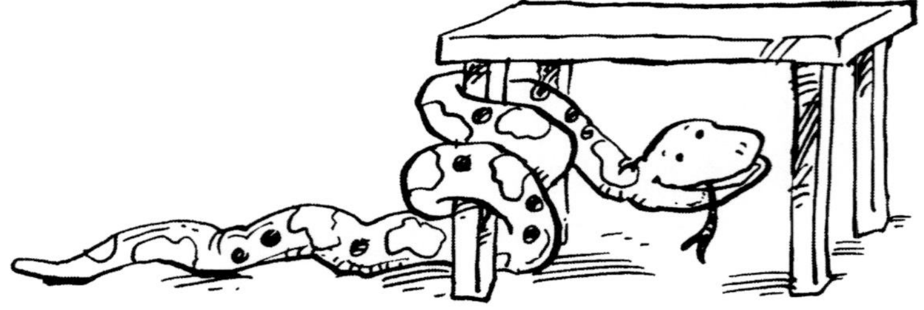

★ How many different ways can the animals sleep now?

Problem Solving Task Card

Finding all the possibilities 33

PROBLEM 33 *Dice doubles*

Numbers 123

Level 1

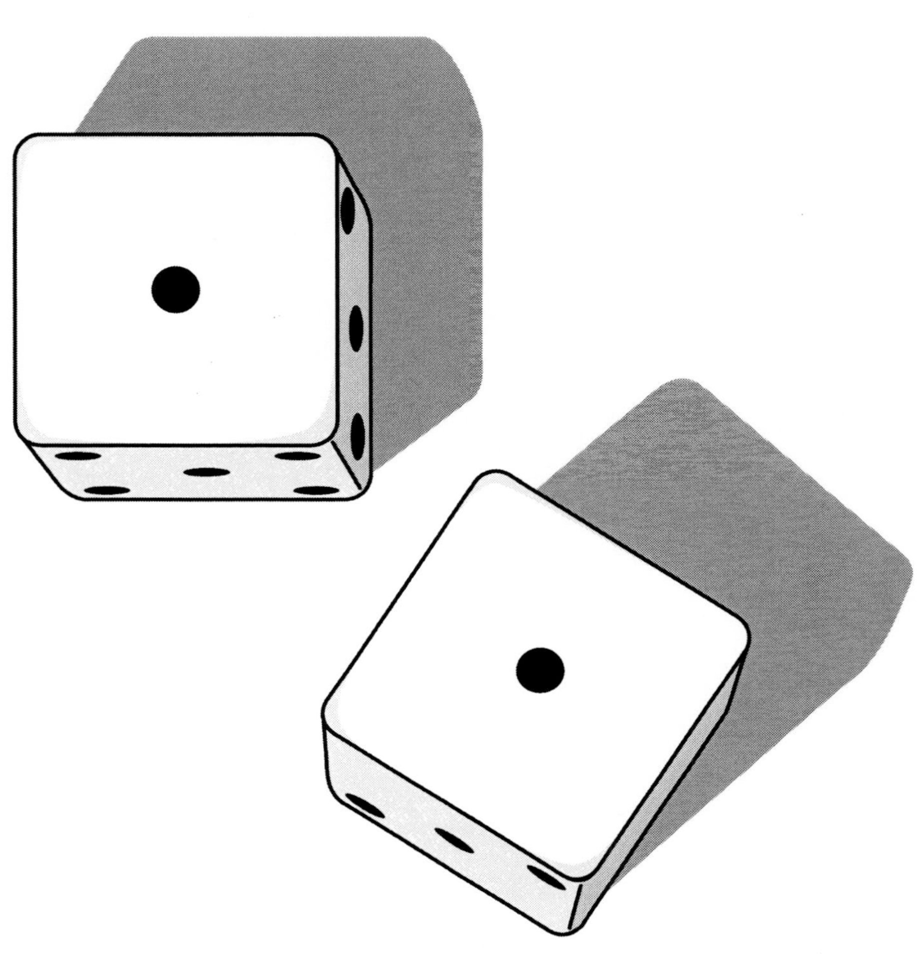

★ What is the total score of these dice?

★ What is special about this score?

★ How many doubles can you score when you throw two dice?

★ How many ways can you score a total that is a double of a number?

Problem 34

Numbers 123

Level 2

Dartboard scores

This dartboard has the numbers 1 to 8.

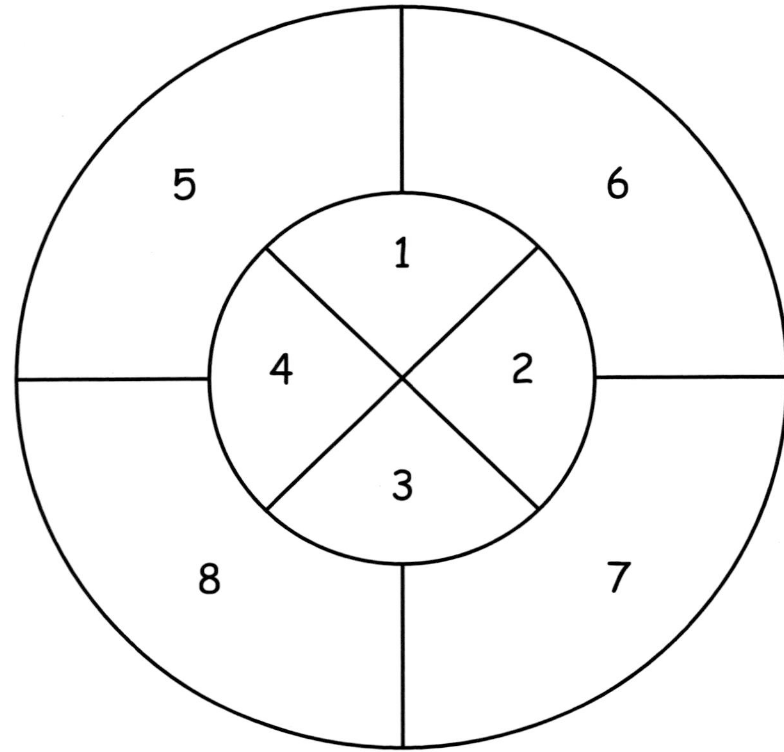

You have two throws. Both darts hit the dartboard.

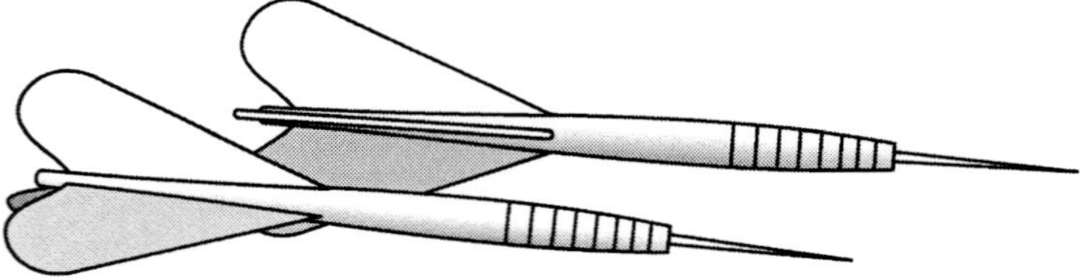

- ★ What could your score be?
- ★ What numbers from 1 to 20 can't you score with two throws?
- ★ How many ways can you score 9 from two throws?

Problem Solving Task Card

Finding all the possibilities 35

PROBLEM 35

Numbers 123

Level 2

Halves

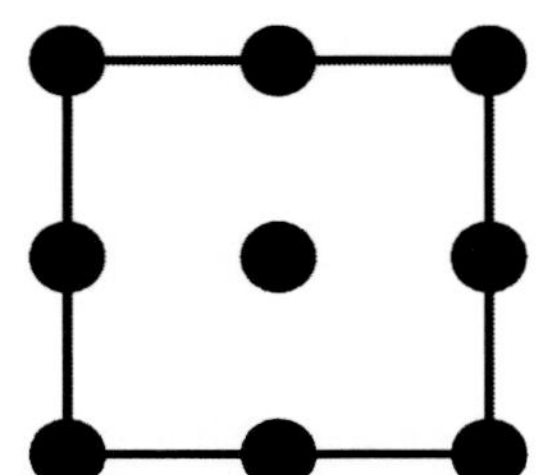

Divide this shape into 2 equal parts.

★ How many more ways can you find to do it?

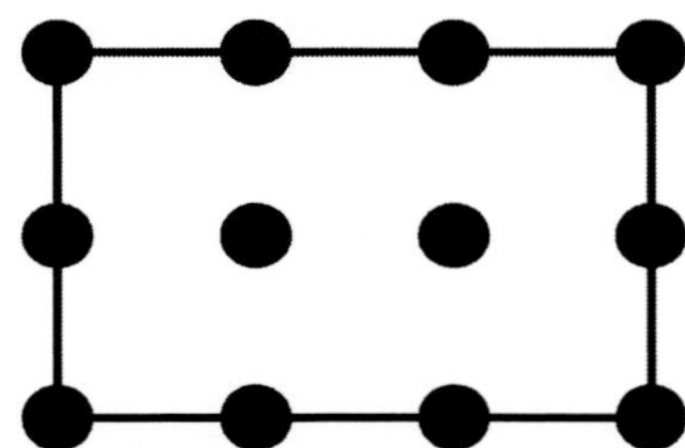

★ Divide this shape into 2 equal parts.

★ How many more ways can you find to do it?

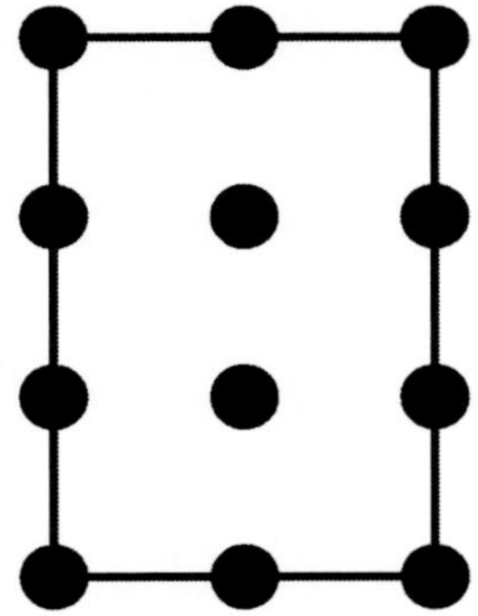

★ How many ways do you think there will be to divide this shape into 2 equal parts?

Problem 36
Buses

Numbers 123

Level 2

Zareena is waiting for a bus to take her home, but she can't remember which buses she can take. She knows that she can take buses that have numbers that fit these clues.

- It is a 2-digit number.
- One digit is double the other.
- It is an even number.

★ Will this bus take Zareena home?

★ What is the number of a bus that will take Zareena home?

Zareena remembers that she can also take buses that have numbers that fit these clues:

- It is a 3-digit number.
- One digit is double another.
- One digit is one quarter of another.

★ How many buses can you find that will take Zareena home?

PROBLEM 37

Numbers 123

Level 2

Pocket money

Mrs Lawlor is giving out pocket money.

This week Mrs Lawlor gives out £22.
She has to remember these pocket money rules.

- Sharon gets more than David.
- She can only give out pound coins.
- There must always be at least £2 difference between the children's pocket money.
- Paul gets less than David.
- Amy gets the least.

How many different ways could Mrs Lawlor share out the pocket money?

PROBLEM 38
2007

Numbers 123

Level 3

2007

★ Using the digits from 2007, how many numbers can you make?

★ Using the digits from 2007 and +, - and = once each time, how many numbers from 0 to 100 can you make?

Level 3

Problem 39

Shape & Space

Make me symmetrical

This shape is not symmetrical.

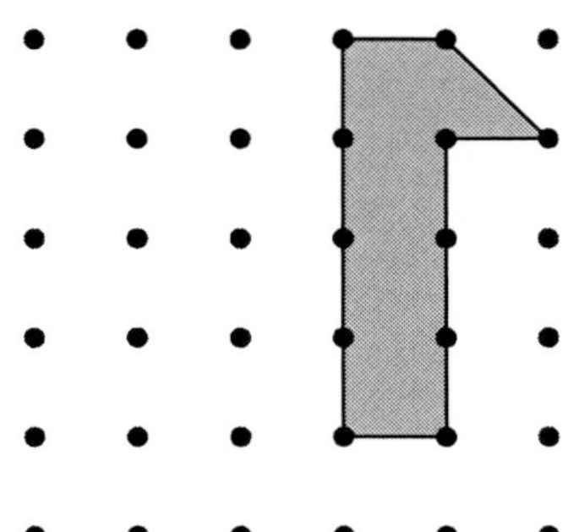

★ Make it into a symmetrical shape.

(You cannot add more squares or half squares than the original shape has.)

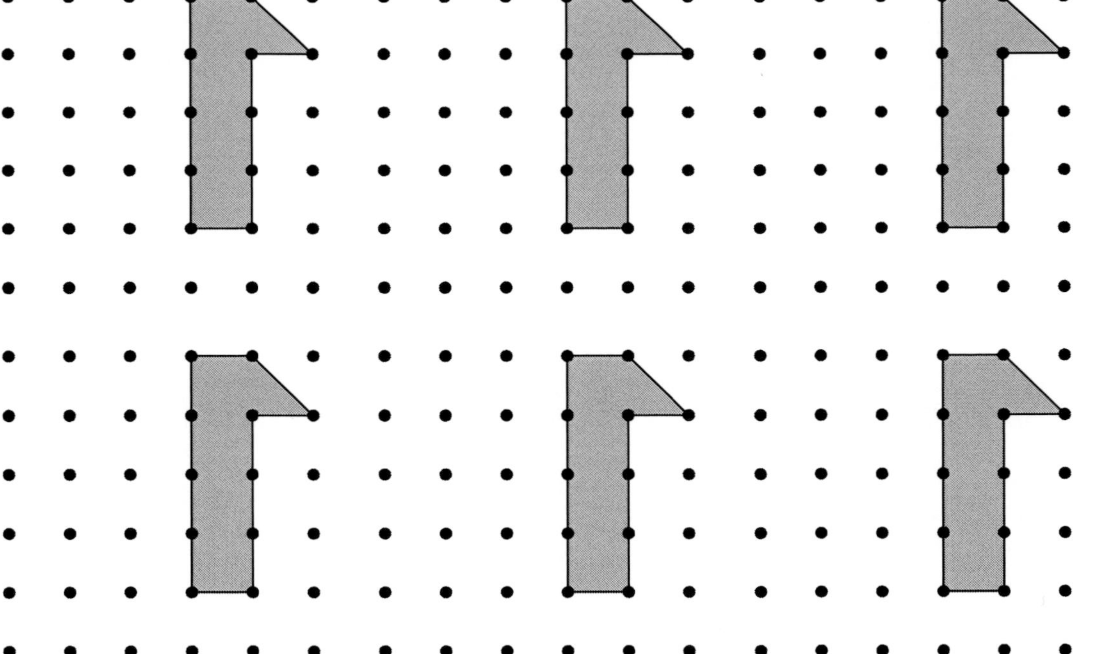

★ How many different ways can you make it into a symmetrical shape?

(Ask for more copies of this page if you need them.)

Level 3

Problem 40

Numbers 123

Missing digits

●, ■ and ♥ each stand for a different digit.

● + ■ = ♥

♥ is bigger than ■.
■ is bigger than ●.

★ What could ●, ■ and ♥ be each time?

★ How many different values can you find for ●, ■ and ♥?

●● + ■■ = ♥♥

★ What could ●●, ■■ and ♥♥ be each time?

★ How many different values can you find for ●●, ■■ and ♥♥?

Finding all the possibilities

PROBLEM 31 *Toys*

Children might find it useful to use Plasticine for this problem or make cardboard cut-outs. They could use one colour to make the parts of the doll, and one colour for the parts of the teddy. Discuss how they could record each combination. Ask children how they know that they have found all the possibilities.

Head - Doll Body - Doll Legs - Doll	Head - Teddy Body - Doll Legs - Doll	Head - Teddy Body - Teddy Legs - Doll	Head - Teddy Body - Doll Legs - Teddy
Head - Teddy Body - Teddy Legs - Teddy	Head - Doll Body - Teddy Legs - Teddy	Head - Doll Body - Doll Legs - Teddy	Head - Doll Body - Teddy Legs - Doll

Extension: How many different toys could you make if you had a toy monster too?

PROBLEM 32 *Bedtime*

Children could record their answers for this by writing the first letter of the animals' names or by drawing pictures. Ask them to check their answers with a friend to ensure that they have the same answers. Discuss whether for this problem 'cat and dog' is the same as 'dog and cat'? (It ought to be.)

dog - cat - rabbit
dog, cat - rabbit
dog, rabbit - cat
cat, rabbit - dog
dog, cat, rabbit

When children come to tackle the second problem, ensure that they realise that the animals could now sleep in two pairs or a pair and two on their own.

dog - cat - rabbit - snake
dog, cat, snake - rabbit
dog, rabbit, snake - cat
cat, rabbit, snake - dog
dog, cat, rabbit - snake
snake, cat - dog - rabbit
snake, rabbit - dog - cat
snake, dog - rabbit - cat
cat, rabbit - dog - snake
cat, dog - rabbit - snake
rabbit, dog - cat - snake
dog, cat - snake, rabbit
dog, rabbit - snake, cat
cat, rabbit - snake, dog
dog, cat, rabbit, snake

Extension: Pete also has three mice: Tiny, Midge and Mini. How many ways could they sleep? Explain your answer.

Finding all the possibilities

PROBLEM 33 *Dice doubles*

Begin this activity by throwing a pair of dice to remind children of the totals that they can score. Children should readily be able to answer the first question. Discuss the second and third questions and ask children to explain their answers. (1 and 1 is a double. There are six ways to score a double: 1 and 1, 2 and 2, 3 and 3, 4 and 4, 5 and 5, 6 and 6.)

When answering the last question, you might want to ask different groups of children to focus on investigating the number of ways to score particular doubles rather than all that are possible. Discuss also whether 1 and 5, and 5 and 1 are different solutions or the same. How do children know when they have found all the possible ways?

1 and 1	1 way only (1 and 1)
2 and 2	2 ways (1 and 3, 2 and 2)
3 and 3	3 ways (1 and 5, 2 and 4, 3 and 3)
4 and 4	3 ways only (2 and 6, 3 and 5, 4 and 4)
5 and 5	2 ways only (4 and 6, 5 and 5)
6 and 6	1 way only (1 and 1)

Can anyone see a pattern in the results?

Extension: How many ways are there to score 7 from throwing two dice?

PROBLEM 34 *Dartboard scores*

Explain that, when the darts are thrown, they could land in two separate sections of the dartboard or in one only. Listen to the scores that children suggest for the first question. Children could work in pairs to answer the second question. Invite children to say how they will find the numbers that can't be made. Highlight those suggestions that involve seeing which scores can be made, and how these numbers might be recorded. The scores that cannot be made are: 1, 17, 18, 19, 20. Ask children to explain their findings. (The highest score that can be made is the double of the highest number on the dartboard: 8 + 8 = 16.)

There are four ways to score 9 (1 and 8, 2 and 7, 3 and 6, 4 and 5).

Extension: Which scores can only be made in one way each?

Finding all the possibilities

PROBLEM 35 *Halves*

Provide dotted grid paper for children to record their answers. Most children will want to divide the shapes into halves by keeping whole small squares. Some children might think of methods that involve dividing the small squares in the shape in half, either diagonally or vertically or horizontally. Ask them to explain why this is possible.

Examples of ways of dividing the first shape into two equal parts:

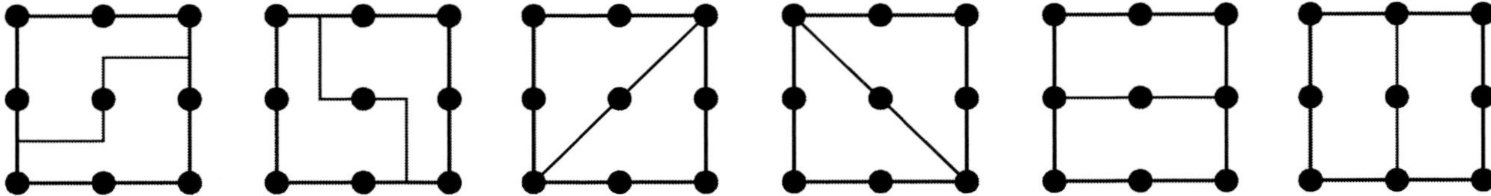

Examples of ways of dividing the second shape into two equal parts:

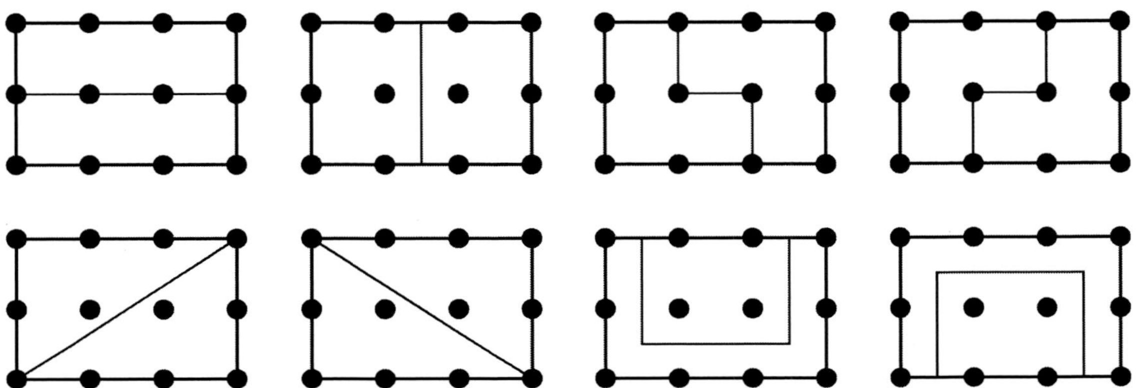

When children have explored splitting the second shape for a little while, they might go back to the first shape with further ideas.

The last question requires children to see that the shape is exactly the same as the second shape.

Extension: How many times can you divide the first shape into four equal parts?

Finding all the possibilities

PROBLEM 36 *Buses*

This problem requires children to use what they know about doubling and halving, and also odd and even numbers. You might want to begin by practising doubling and halving, and recognising odd and even numbers.

Zareena can't take the bus in the picture. It has a digit that is double another (8 is double 4), and it is even, but it has three digits. These are the buses that Zareena would be able to take:

12, 24, 42, 36, 48, 84

Ask children to explain why numbers like 21 and 63 can't be Zareena's buses.

The answers to the last question are:

124, 142, 214, 241, 412, 421   248, 284, 428, 482, 824, 842

Discuss why for this problem 124 is different to 142. How do children know when they have found all the answers?

Extension: Daniel can take a bus home with numbers that fit these clues:

- It is a 2-digit number.
- There is a difference of 3 between the digits.
- It is odd.

How many buses can Daniel take home?

PROBLEM 37 *Pocket money*

Children could use plastic money or counters to help them with this problem, and could work in groups of four, with each child taking the part of one of the children in the picture. Check that they understand the pocket money rules. Discuss the ways that they could record their answers to the problem.

Amy	Paul	David	Sharon
£1	£3	£5	£13
£1	£3	£6	£12
£1	£3	£7	£11
£1	£3	£8	£10
£1	£4	£6	£11
£1	£4	£7	£10
£1	£5	£7	£9
£2	£4	£6	£10
£2	£4	£7	£9

Extension: The Stuart children share £18 pocket money between Aleysha, Ben and Craig. Ben and Craig are twins so they always get the same amount. Aleysha is the youngest, so she gets less than they do.

How many ways can the money be shared?

Finding all the possibilities

PROBLEM 38 *2007*

Discuss whether a number can begin with 0. On the board, list examples of 4-digit, 3-digit, 2-digit and 1-digit numbers that children can make, e.g. 2007 itself, 270, 70 and 7. While children are working, check that they remember that 0 can be used in the middle of numbers as well as at the end.

Numbers that can be made from 2, 0, 0 and 7:

0	20	200	2007
2	70	207	2070
7	27	270	2700
	72	700	7002
		702	7020
		720	7200

Numbers from 0 to 100 that can be made using the digits from 2007 and +, - and =.

0 + 0 = 0	20 + 0 = 20	7 - 2 = 5	20 - 7 = 13
0 + 2 = 2	20 + 7 = 27	7 - 7 = 0	20 - 0 = 20
0 + 7 = 7	70 + 0 = 70	2 - 2 = 0	70 - 2 = 68
2 + 7 = 9	70 + 2 = 72		70 - 20 = 50
			70 - 0 = 70

Extension: How many numbers can you make from 0 to 100 using the digits from 2007 and +, +, - and =?

PROBLEM 39 *Make me symmetrical*

This problem could have an infinite number of solutions, so it is important to limit it in some way to prevent answers that lead to:

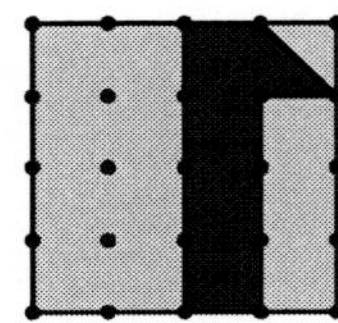

Provide mirrors for children to check their answers if necessary.

These are the possible answers to the problem with the constraint that the shape cannot be more than doubled in size:

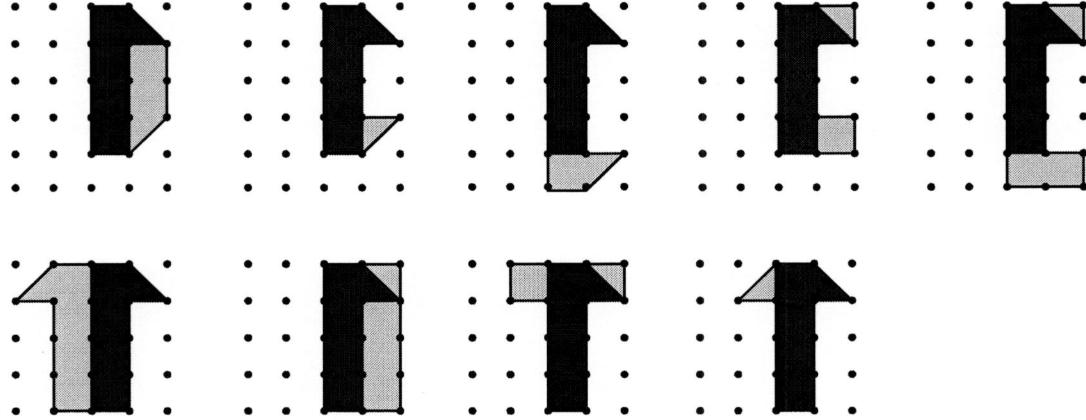

Finding all the possibilities

PROBLEM 40 *Missing digits*

Ask children to explain what they think is meant by this problem, as it is important to check that they understand that ●, ■ and ♥ are different digits, and that each time a symbol is used the digit it stands for must be used. An answer is made up of a set of three digits, e.g. ● = 1, ■ = 2 and ♥ = 3. In the second part of the activity, it is necessary that children realise that the problem is asking for 2-digit numbers as answers. As there are so many possibilities, children could work in pairs to find the answers. Discuss with them how they can record their answers systematically so that they make sure that they find them all. For children who need more support, you could say that ♥ is less than 6.

Answers to the first question:

1 + 2 = 3 1 + 3 = 4 1 + 4 = 5 1 + 5 = 6 1 + 6 = 7 1 + 7 = 8 1 + 8 = 9
2 + 3 = 5 2 + 4 = 6 2 + 5 = 7 2 + 6 = 8 2 + 7 = 9
3 + 4 = 7 3 + 5 = 8 3 + 6 = 9
4 + 5 = 9

When children come to answer the second question, look to see who sees the connection with the answers to the first question. If any children are still working the answers out from scratch, invite other children to explain why they don't have to. (The answers to the second question can all be found by adding extra digits to the answers to the first question, because when adding these numbers of tens and units you will always get the same number of tens and units in the answer.)

Answers to the second question:

11 + 22 = 33 11 + 33 = 44 11 + 44 = 55 11 + 55 = 66
11 + 66 = 77 11 + 77 = 88 11 + 88 = 99

22 + 33 = 55 22 + 44 = 66 22 + 55 = 77 22 + 66 = 88
22 + 77 = 99

33 + 44 = 77 33 + 55 = 88 33 + 66 = 99
44 + 55 = 99

Extension: What are the possible answers to ●●● + ■■■ = ♥♥♥?

Using a table

Solve THAT PROBLEM!

Solve THAT PROBLEM!

Solve THAT PROBLEM!

Using a table

Tables and charts are used in many different ways in maths. Their main purpose is to organise information. Often this is information that has been collected as a result of a survey or a vote of hands, and the data that is contained in a table can then be analysed and interpreted. Teaching example 1 follows this pattern. However, children can also use tables to organise their answers to a problem or to help them see the relationships between different aspects of a problem. Teaching example 2 shows how children can record their results in a table and so identify a pattern.

TEACHING EXAMPLE 1

These are the activities a group of children did at a holiday camp on one day.

How many children played football in the afternoon?

	Morning	Afternoon
Claire	Swimming	Football
John	Football	Swimming
Sita	Football	Tennis
Ekou	Tennis	Football
Josh	Swimming	Tennis

Understand the problem

What do we know?
We know who did what activity in the morning and in the afternoon.

What do we need to find out?
Who were the children who played football?
Who played football in the afternoon?

Make a plan

What we did
Invite children to look at the table and say what they can tell from it. Ask children to break down the question and to tell you how many things you need to know to be able to answer it. Highlight the fact that they need to be thinking about two things: they need to think about the number of children who played football, but not all the children who played football. They have to look for the children who played football in the afternoon.

Ask a volunteer to ring the information in the table that will give the answer.

2 children played football in the afternoon.

Discuss how different this answer is to the number of children who played football altogether, or the number of times children played football.

	Morning	Afternoon
Claire	Swimming	(Football)
John	Football	Swimming
Sita	Football	Tennis
Ekou	Tennis	(Football)
Josh	Swimming	Tennis

Reflect

Children will see that sometimes a table can give you more information than simply what is the most common event or who did what. They need to think carefully about questions and make sure that they answer each part of it.

Support

Children could say how many times children in the group played football.

Extension

Children could find the difference between the number of children who played football in the morning compared with the afternoon.

Using a table

TEACHING EXAMPLE 2

On Monday there were 10 apples, 50 cherries and 20 bananas in Jo's house. On Tuesday there were 9 apples, 45 cherries and 18 bananas. On Wednesday there were 8 apples, 40 cherries and 16 bananas. How many will be left of each on Sunday?

Understand the problem

What do we know?

On Monday there were 10 apples, 50 cherries and 20 bananas.
On Tuesday there were 9 apples, 45 cherries and 18 bananas.
On Wednesday there were 8 apples, 40 cherries and 16 bananas.

What do we need to find out?

How much of each fruit is eaten every day?

Make a plan

What we did

Draw the table below on the board, writing in the information that is known from the question.

Ask children to look at the apples. How many apples do they think will be there on Thursday? Why? Repeat for the cherries and the bananas, encouraging children to describe what is happening to the numbers as they go down the column (number of apples going down by 1, number of cherries going down by 5, number of bananas going down by 2, every day).

	Apples	**Cherries**	**Bananas**
Monday	10	50	20
Tuesday	9	45	18
Wednesday	8	40	16
Thursday			
Friday			
Saturday			
Sunday			

Ask children to work out how much fruit will be left on Sunday by subtracting 1, 5 or 2 for every day from Thursday to Sunday. Fill in the table.

	Apples	**Cherries**	**Bananas**
Monday	10	50	20
Tuesday	9	45	18
Wednesday	8	40	16
Thursday	7	35	14
Friday	6	30	12
Saturday	5	25	10
Sunday	4	20	8

Reflect

Children will be able to see that putting information in a table can help you see relationships more clearly.

Support

Children could carry out the same investigation but for one fruit at a time.

Extension

Children could also find out how many satsumas will be left on Sunday. There were 25 on Monday, 22 on Tuesday, 19 on Wednesday.

Problem Solving Task Card

Using a table 41

PROBLEM 41

Numbers 123

Level 1

Names and letters

This table shows the length of the names of Ruby's pets.

Name	Number of letters
Princess	
Cat	3
Fluffy	
Ginger	
Flash	
Gordon	

- ★ Fill in the missing numbers.
- ★ Whose name is the longest?
- ★ Whose name has 1 letter fewer than Fluffy?
- ★ Whose names have the same number of letters as Gordon?
- ★ Cat is short for Catherine. What can you say about the longest name now?
- ★ Ruby has a gerbil called Jane. Write her name and number of letters in the table.

Problem 42

Numbers 1 2 3

Level 1

Dice scores 1

You need four children to play with and two dice.

★ Write your names in the table.

Name	First dice score	Second dice score	Total score

★ Take it in turns to roll the two dice. Add your scores. Write the total in the table.

★ Whose total score was the highest?

★ Whose score was lowest?

★ Whose scores were between the highest and the lowest?

★ Play the game again.

Name	First dice score	Second dice score	Total score

★ Who had the greatest difference between their scores for the two games?

PROBLEM 43
Numbers 1 2 3

Level 1

Dice scores 2

These children played a game.
They rolled the dice and added their scores.

This table shows their totals.

Name	Total
Alice	5
Brian	7
Cara	
Dinesh	4
Eleme	12

Cara's total was less than Eleme's total and more than Brian's total.

★ What could her total have been?

★ What numbers could have been on her dice to make this total?

★ What other totals could she have had?
Write your answers in this table.

Total	Score on black dice	Score on white dice

Problem Solving Task Card
Using a table 44

PROBLEM 44

Numbers 123

Level 2

Candles

Today is Bob and Jane's birthday and they each have a cake. Grandma has ten candles to put on the cakes.

★ How old could Bob and Jane be?

Write your answers in the table.

Bob	Jane

★ Look at your answers and think about this information.

- Bob and Jane are not twins.
- Bob is younger than Jane.
- Jane's age is not an even number.
- Next year Bob will be half Jane's age.

★ How old are Bob and Jane?

Level 2

PROBLEM 45

Numbers 123

Chocolate chunks

Jake and Matt are twins.

When they share a bar of chocolate, one twin has half, then the other twin has half of what's left, and so on. When there are fewer than 5 pieces left, they give what's left to their sister, Gloria.

★ Fill in this table for a bar of chocolate with 48 pieces.
Jake has the first half.
The first part is done for you.

Jake	Matt	Gloria
24	0	0

★ Fill in this table for a bar of chocolate with 48 pieces.
Matt has the first half.

Matt	Jake	Gloria
24	0	0

★ How many pieces does each twin get to eat each time?

★ Does it matter who goes first?

★ Is this a fair way for the twins to share the chocolate?

PROBLEM 46

Handling data

Level 2

Ice cream and lollies

This chart shows the snacks Katy and Max had when they were on holiday.

	Katy	Max
Monday		CRISPS
Tuesday	CRISPS	CRISPS
Wednesday		
Thursday		
Friday		
Saturday		
Sunday		CRISPS

- ★ How many more times did Katy have an ice cream than Max?
- ★ How many times did the children have an ice cream during the week?
- ★ Who do you think likes crisps more? Katy or Max? Why?
- ★ Katy's mum had twice as many ice creams as Katy did. How many did Katy's mum eat?
- ★ How many times did Max have a lolly?
- ★ On what day was the picture taken?
- ★ Lollies cost 95p and ice creams cost £1. How much more did Max and Katy spend on their ice creams during the week?

Level 2

PROBLEM 47

Numbers 123

Theme park

Jo is at the theme park.

Jo has 10 tokens. She wants to use as many tokens as she can, but she can only go on each ride once.

★ Which of the rides can she go on? Use the table to help you.

(You might not need all the rows.)

Splash buggy 4 tokens	Whirligig 2 tokens	Upside down flyer 7 tokens	Ghost train 5 tokens	Bat lift 1 token	Tokens used	Tokens left
4	2	-------	-------	1	7	3

★ If you were Jo, what rides would you go on?

PROBLEM 48

Numbers 123

Level 3

Twenty-one

In the game 'Twenty-one', you are aiming to score 21 or to get less than 21. If you get more than 21, you are out.

An ace is worth 1 or 11 and a king, queen or a jack is worth 10.

Billy has 14. He can take another card or he can stick at 14.

★ What totals might he get? Use the table to help you.

Card number	Total
Ace	
2	
3	
4	
5	
6	
7	
8	
9	
10	
King	
Queen	
Jack	

★ Billy knows that all the picture cards, the 9s and the 10s have been used. Should he ask for another card or should he stick? Why?

Remember: highest score wins. As long as it is not higher than 21!

Level 3

PROBLEM 49

Numbers 1 2 3

Construction kit

Jin and Louise have 24 wheels in their construction kit.

They are making cars and motorbikes.

Jin makes the motorbikes.
Louise makes cars with 4 wheels.

★ How many wheels can they each have? Use this table to help you.

Jin's wheels	Louise's wheels
0	
2	
4	
6	
8	
10	
12	
14	
16	
18	
20	
22	
24	

★ How many motorbikes and cars can they make?

★ Louise uses half the wheels that Jin does.
How many motorbikes and cars do they make?

Problem 50 Numbers 123 Level 3

Toe prints

Last night there were strange creatures about...

All that was left in the morning were toe prints.

All the animals walked on two feet.

Saggybods have 2 toes on each foot.
Coolpeeps have 1 toe on each foot.
Dunewods have 5 toes on each foot.

There were 20 toe prints in the mud.

★ How many saggybods, coolpeeps and dunewods were there? Use the table to help you. One has been done for you.

Saggybods		Coolpeeps		Dunewods	
Number of toes	Number of Saggybods	Number of toes	Number of Coolpeeps	Number of toes	Number of Dunewods
20	5	0	0	0	0

Using a table

PROBLEM 41 *Names and letters*

Prepare children to use a table by drawing one on the board and asking children to count how many letters are in their names. They can then fill in a row on the table for themselves.

Name	Number of letters
Princess	8
Cat	3
Fluffy	6
Ginger	6
Flash	5
Gordon	6
Jane	4

Extension: Fill in a table for the names of the pets you know.

PROBLEMS 42 AND 43 *Dice scores 1 and 2*

These two activities are linked. They use the same context and build up to children using a table to organise their answers. In **Problem 42 Dice scores 1**, children play a dice game where they total scores. They write their scores in a table and answer questions about their results. You might want to practice this game as a group first, before children play on their own. For **Problem 43 Dice scores 2**, children could work in pairs to find out Cara's possible total and the dice scores that made it. Discuss with them how they can use the table to record their answers. Cara's total could have been 8, 9, 10 or 11. In this problem, 2 and 6 is different to 6 and 2 because two different dice were used.

Total	Score on black dice	Score on white dice
8	2	6
8	6	2
8	3	5
8	5	3
8	4	4
9	3	6
9	6	3
10	5	5
11	6	5
11	5	6

Extension: Brian's next total was more than half Dinesh' first total, but less than double Alice's first total. What could it have been?

Using a table

PROBLEM 44 *Candles*

Discuss how children can use the table to record their answers. Explain that they can write Bob's age in the table, subtract that number from 10 to work out Jane's age and then write that in the table.

Bob	Jane
9	1
8	2
7	3
6	4
5	5
4	6
3	7
2	8
1	9

In the second part of the activity, children use their tables to help them work out Bob and Jane's ages. They aren't twins so they can't be 5 and 5. Bob is younger so Jane can't be less than 6. Jane's age is odd so they are either 3 and 7 or 1 and 9. Next year Bob will be half Jane's age. They are 3 and 7.

Ask children how they think that writing their answers in a table helped them when they tackled the second part of the activity.

Extension: Bob and Jane's big sister is less than ten times as old as Bob but more than twice as old as Jane. How old could she be?

PROBLEM 45 *Chocolate chunks*

Explain how children should record their answers in the tables.

Jake	Matt	Gloria
24	0	0
0	12	0
6	0	0
0	0	3

Matt	Jake	Gloria
24	0	0
0	12	0
6	0	0
0	0	3

Discuss whether this is a fair way for the chocolate to be shared. Listen to children's views for and against and ask them to justify them, e.g. some children might feel that if the twins take turns each time, then it is fair as they will get to eat the same amount of chocolate every two turns (as long as the chocolate bars are the same size).

Extension: Is it always better to be the child who starts? Try the problem for bars of chocolate with 64, 36 and 24 pieces. How many pieces of chocolate must there be for the twin who goes second not to get any chocolate?

Using a table

PROBLEM 46 *Ice cream and lollies*

The problems on this task card require children to use all the information that they are given. To answer the sixth question, children have to use the table and the picture to find the information they need. Before children begin, check that they understand:

- Katy had an ice cream once more than Max.
- The children had ice creams five times.
- Max had crisps three times compared to Katy's once, so he probably likes them more than she does.
- Katy's mum had six ice creams.
- Max had a lolly twice.
- The picture was taken on Friday (it shows Katy eating a lolly and Max eating an ice cream).
- □Ice creams cost 5p more than lollies. They had 5 lollies and 5 ice creams between them. They spent 25p (5 × 5p) more on ice creams during the week.

PROBLEM 47 *Theme park*

Check that children understand that Jo doesn't want to have any tokens left over unless she has to. Therefore she wouldn't go only on the Splash buggy (4 tokens) and the Ghost train (5 tokens) because she could still use 1 token on the Bat lift. Ask children to explain why, in the example on the task sheet, Jo can't use the 3 tokens. (She has already been on the Whirligig and the Bat lift and she hasn't got enough for the other rides.)

Splash buggy 4 tokens	Whirligig 2 tokens	Upside down flyer 7 tokens	Ghost train 5 tokens	Bat lift 1 token	Tokens used	Tokens left
4	2	———	———	1	7	3
4	———	———	5	1	10	0
———	2	7	———	1	10	0
———	2	———	5	1	8	2
———	———	7	———	1	8	2

Ask children for their answers to the last question, and discuss their reasons.

Extension: Jo's brother gives her 2 more tokens. What rides could Jo go on now?

Using a table

PROBLEM 48 *Twenty-one*

Show children a pack of cards before this activity. Explain that, instead of a card with 1 on it, there are aces, and that in the game of 'Twenty-one' you can choose whether an ace is worth 1 or 11. You might want to play the game a few times first to help children understand the context. Each child receives two cards and they add them. They don't show anyone else what they have got. They decide whether to take another card or to stick. You cannot stick if you have a score less than 11. The aim of the game is to be closer to 21 than anyone else but not to go above it.

Card number	Total
Ace	15
2	16
3	17
4	18
5	19
6	20
7	21
8	22
9	23
10	24
King	24
Queen	24
Jack	24

Without the picture cards, 9s or 10s, Billy is more likely to get a card that gives him a total that is less than 21 than above it. Listen to children's ideas as to the answer of the last question and ask them to justify their decisions.

PROBLEM 49 *Construction kit*

Explain that, to solve the problem, children need to think about how many lots of 2 and 4 the children have. The table on the task card helps children to organise the possible ways that the wheels might be shared. When they have completed it, ask them to think about the second question.

Jin's wheels	Louise's wheels
0	24
2	22
4	20
6	18
8	16
10	14
12	12
14	10
16	8
18	6
20	4
22	2
24	0

If necessary, remind children that Louise needs 4 wheels each time for a car. From the table, it's clear to see that the possible solutions are:

Louise 6 cars and Jin 0 motorbikes
Louise 5 cars and Jin 2 motorbikes
Louise 4 cars and Jin 4 motorbikes
Louise 3 cars and Jin 6 motorbikes
Louise 2 cars and Jin 8 motorbikes
Louise 1 car and Jin 10 motorbikes
Louise 0 cars and Jin 12 motorbikes

The final information shows that Louise makes 2 cars (8 wheels) and Jin makes 8 motorbikes (16 wheels).

Extension: Trevor wants to make tricycles. How many tricycles and cars can he and Louise make?

Using a table

PROBLEM 50 *Toe prints*

This activity uses multiplication facts for the 2, 4, and 10 times tables. You might want to start by practising these facts. When children are solving this problem, check that they remember to double the number of toes each time to work out the number of animals – all the animals have two feet. Consequently 4 toes could be one Saggybod, 2 toes could be 1 Coolpeep, and 10 toes could be 1 Dunewod. Remind them that the total has to be 20 each time. Children might find it useful to use cubes to help them share out the numbers of toes.

Saggybods		Coolpeeps		Dunewods	
Number of toes	**Number of Saggybods**	**Number of toes**	**Number of Coolpeeps**	**Number of toes**	**Number of Dunewods**
20	5	0	0	0	0
16	4	4	2	0	0
12	3	8	4	0	0
8	2	12	6	0	0
8	2	2	1	10	1
4	1	16	8	0	0
4	1	6	3	10	1
0	0	20	10	0	0
0	0	10	5	10	1
0	0	0	0	20	2

Extension: Coolpeeps are timid and only go out in groups of five. Dunewods always hunt in packs of three. Saggybods only ever go out in pairs. Use this information to work out how many animals were out last night and what they were. (10 Coolpeeps)

Assessment activities

Solve
THAT PROBLEM!

Solve
THAT PROBLEM!

Assessment activities

These activities could be used as part of your end-of-year teacher assessment. In this section, children have to decide for themselves how to solve the problems, choosing the strategy or strategies that are most appropriate for a particular question.

The problems progress in difficulty. You might like to work one-to-one with children who are at Level 1 and record their answers for them. The notes below give the answers to the problems, explain the most efficient methods that children could use to solve them, and highlight any issues to look out for.

Problem A1

Children have to count the number of candles and say one more than it to give Sam's age. This requires them to understand that 1 year older means the same as 1 year more.

The correct answer is 7. Children who write 6 did not remember that they had to give Sam's age and not David's.

Problem A2

This question requires children to be able to identify shapes when they are not in their usual positions and also to be able to recognise a pattern. Children could have drawn out that section of the pattern to help them.

The correct answer is the square. Look out for children who tick the kite or the rectangle. They have recognised the pattern, but failed to identify the shapes on the mobile as squares. Children who tick the circle have not understood the pattern.

Problem A3

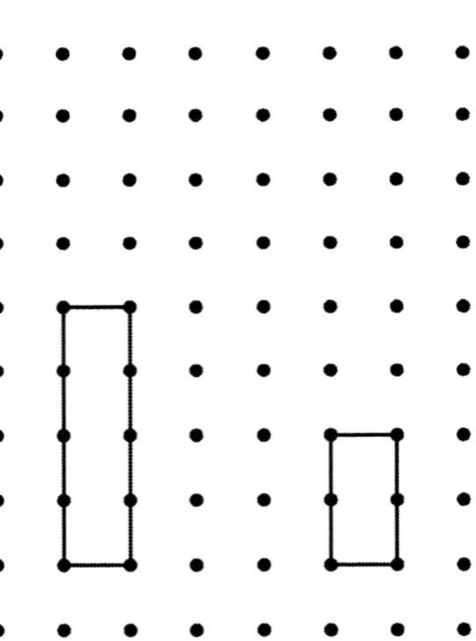

Children will need rulers for this question. They have to halve the height of the rectangle and then draw their own rectangle (2cm long) on the grid.

The answer is a rectangle 2cm long.

Children who draw a rectangle 8cm long have doubled instead of halving. Children who draw a rectangle wider than the one given but 2cm long can still get a mark as they have followed the instruction.

Problem A4

Children read information from a table to answer the two parts of this question. The first question requires them to total the goal scores for each school and compare them. For the second question, children need to use new information with the table to find the answer.

The answers are:

1 5
2 6

Assessment activities

PROBLEM A5

This problem requires children to find different ways of making 54 with two-digit numbers, and then to choose from these ways those that match with the digits shown and that give different digits for the boxes.

Possible solutions are:

27 + 27 = 54 (this is the only solution for this calculation)
35 + 19 = 54
39 + 15 = 54
38 + 16 = 54
36 + 18 = 34

When answering the second calculation, children who write 7 twice have not appreciated that they need to write different digits.

Check children's working for this question. Encourage those who have shown little or no working to look at those who have recorded possibilities systematically as if in a table (even if they haven't actually drawn one).

PROBLEM A6

For this question, children have to show a correct method to get the answer. They could draw 85 cherries and split them into fives, or show 5 being added repeatedly. If drawing, it is important that they show how the symbols could be partitioned into fifteens or fives.

These are examples of correct responses:

5 + 5 + 5 + 5 + 5 + 5 + 5
5 10 15 20 25 30 35
5 + 5 + 5 + 5 + 5 + 5 + 5
40 45 50 55 60 65 70
5 + 5 + 5
75 80 85

(00000) *5*	*5* (00000)	*5* (00000)
(00000) *5*	*5* (00000)	*5* (00000)
(00000) *5*	*5* (00000)	*5* (00000)
(00000) *5*	*5* (00000)	*5* (00000)
(00000) *5*	*5* (00000)	*5* (00000)
(00000) *5*	*5* (00000)	

PROBLEM A7

To answer this question correctly, children must be able to recognise the shape that is created when triangles have been cut off a six-pointed star.

The answer is a hexagon.

Look out for children who answer the question (whether correctly or incorrectly) without drawing on the diagram. Talk through the problem afterwards and invite them to see how much easier it is to work out the answer when they can see the shape on the page.

Problem Solving Task Card

Assessment activities A1

PROBLEM A1

Level 1

This is David's birthday cake.

Sam is 1 year **older** than David.

How old is Sam?

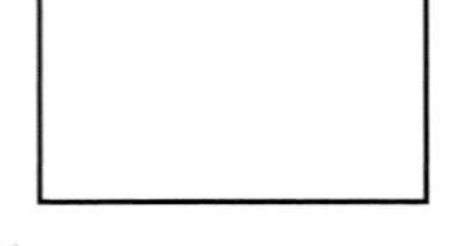

years

Level 1

PROBLEM A2

A shape has fallen off the mobile.

What is the shape?
Tick (✓) it.

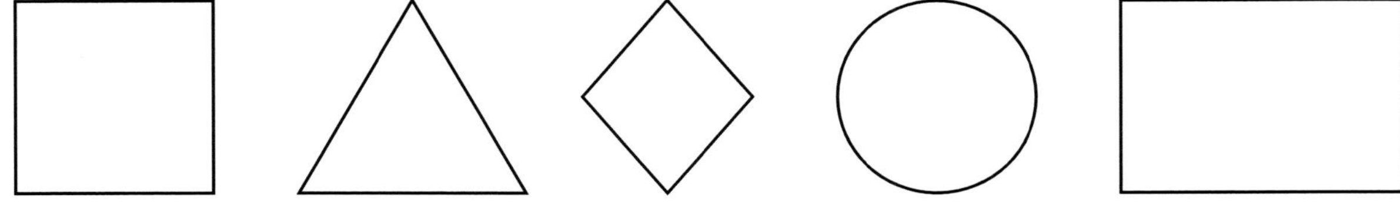

Level 2

PROBLEM A3

Draw a rectangle half as tall as the rectangle shown.

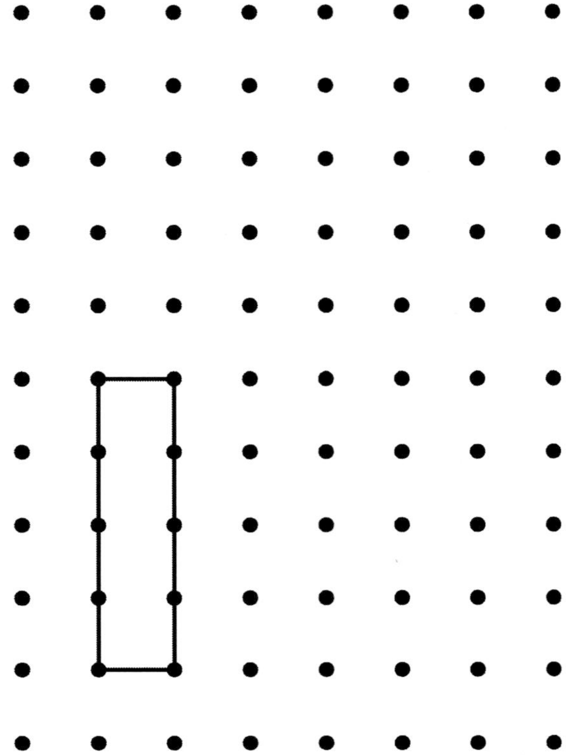

Problem Solving Task Card

Assessment activities

A4

PROBLEM A4

Level 2

The chart shows the goals scored each day at a football camp.

	Hill School	Dale School
Tuesday	5	2
Wednesday	0	6
Thursday	2	1
Friday	3	4
Saturday	1	3

1 How many more goals did Dale School score than Hill School?

2 At the weekend, Hill School scored 7 goals.

How many goals did they score on Sunday?

Level 2

PROBLEM A5

Write four **different** digits to make these correct.

2		+		7	=	5	4
3		+	1		=	5	4

Assessment activities A6

PROBLEM A6

Level 3

Mrs Low had 85 cherries. She shared them equally between 5 children. She gave each child 17 cherries.

Show how Mrs Low could have worked out how many cherries to give to each child.

PROBLEM A7

Level 3

Ben has a star.

He cut a triangle of this size off each corner.

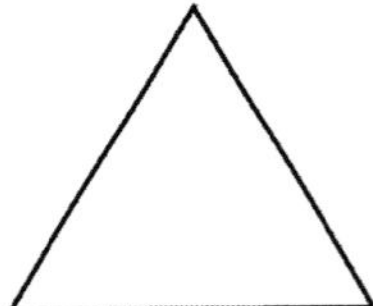

What is the name of the shape that is left?

Tick (✓) it:

- pentagon ☐
- hexagon ☐
- heptagon ☐
- octagon ☐
- decagon ☐

Class . . . .

Problem Solving Task Record Sheet

Task	Level	Name																																
1 Staircase	1																																	
2 Wonder worm	1																																	
3 Birthday badges	1																																	
4 Initials	2																																	
5 Slime	2																																	
6 Picnic panic	2																																	
7 Harold & cabbages	2																																	
8 Give a dog a bone	3																																	
9 Goldilocks' porridge	3																																	
10 Matchstick squares	3																																	
11 Classroom tables	1																																	
12 Jugglers	1																																	
13 Rabbit runs	1																																	
14 Super Baby	2																																	
15 Postman's walk	2																																	
16 Nut stores	2																																	
17 Snail trails	2																																	
18 How many dots?	3																																	
19 Home to the ant hill	3																																	
20 Incy's weather	3																																	
21 Necklaces	1																																	
22 The marble monster	1																																	
23 Digit duos	1																																	
24 100-square puzzle	2																																	
25 New Year kisses	2																																	
26 Pyramid puzzles	2																																	
27 Mr Blake's washing	2																																	
28 Triangle patterns	3																																	
29 Calculator digits	3																																	
30 Charlie's choices	3																																	
31 Toys	1																																	
32 Bedtime	1																																	
33 Dice doubles	1																																	
34 Dartboard scores	2																																	
35 Halves	2																																	
36 Buses	2																																	
37 Pocket money	2																																	
38 2007	3																																	
39 Make me symmetrica	3																																	
40 Missing digits	3																																	
41 Names & letters	1																																	
42 Dice scores 1	1																																	
43 Dice sores 2	1																																	
44 Candles	2																																	
45 Chocolate chunks	2																																	
46 Ice cream & lollies	2																																	
47 Theme park	2																																	
48 Twenty-one	3																																	
49 Construction kit	3																																	
50 Toe prints	3																																	
Assessment 1	1																																	
Assessment 2	1																																	
Assessment 3	2																																	
Assessment 4	2																																	
Assessment 5	2																																	
Assessment 6	3																																	
Assessment 7	3																																	

Badger Publishing Limited
15 Wedgwood Gate
Pin Green Industrial Estate
Stevenage, Hertfordshire SG1 4SU
Telephone: 01438 356907
Fax: 01438 747015
www.badger-publishing.co.uk
enquiries@badger-publishing.co.uk

Badger Maths Problem Solving
Years 1-2

First published 2007
ISBN 978-1-84691-206-1

Publisher: David Jamieson
Editor: Paul Martin
Designer: Adam Wilmott
Illustrator: Juliet Breese & Adam Wilmott

Printed in the UK